SELL
YOUR
JEWELRY

SELL

YOUR

JEWELRY

How to Start a Jewelry
Business and Make Money
Selling Jewelry

AT BOUTIQUES FAIRS TRUNK SHOWS ETSY

By Stacie Vander Pol

pac ps

Pacific Publishing Studio

Published in the United States by Madrona Books, an imprint of Pacific
Publishing Studio.
www.PacPS.com

ISBN – 978-0-9823756-0-0

To order a copy of this book, visit www.Amazon.com.

Cover Photography: iStock Photo, Jaap2

Table of Contents

Chapter 1: A Jewelry Business..................................... 1

Chapter 2: Style and Niche 7

   Define Your Style 8

   Develop a Niche 10

Chapter 3: Know Your Customer................................. 15

   Define Your Target Customer 16

Chapter 4: Professionalism 25

   Personal Professionalism 26

   Policies... 31

   Professional Presentation 35

Chapter 5: Pricing 37

   Components of Pricing 38

   Determining the Price 40

   Increase the Value of Your Jewelry 42

Chapter 6: Presentation 46

   Packaging... 47

   Display 49

   Promotional Words 52

   One Product Five Ways 53

Chapter 7: Making the Sale (Part 1)............................. 59

   Open House 60

   Home Parties 64

   Online Sales at Etsy.com 71

Chapter 8: Making the Sale (Part 2) 75

    Markets, Street Fairs, and Craft Shows 76

    Boutiques and Other Retail Outlets 79

    Trunk Shows 83

    Consignment 85

Chapter 9: Your Business 89

    Making Yourself Official 90

    Business Goals 98

Chapter 10: Lower Costs and Higher Profits 103

    Cost of Time.. 105

    Cost of Materials 108

Chapter 11: Business Operations 115

    Your Process 116

    Inventory 117

    Order Fulfillment 122

Chapter 12: Tax Deductions 125

    Tax Reporting 126

    Tax Deducting... 126

Appendix 135

    Gem and Jewelry Suppliers and Expos........................ 135

Index.. 143

1

A Jewelry Business

When you find a hobby you love, it's easy to imagine it as a full-time career. Through years of jewelry crafting, I've had the opportunity to meet people from many walks of life who've successfully turned their passion for handmade jewelry into a profitable business venture. Though starting a business is challenging, the pursuit of a dream can be deeply gratifying. An endeavor that starts with a few pieces of jewelry and a small dream can become a journey that inspires passion and rewards determination. Those who succeed are incredibly committed to the craft and devoted to working hard at it every day.

From architects to hairstylists and every profession in between, America boasts over ten million people who work for themselves. Owning a business is one of the foundations of the American dream. When met with discipline and self-motivation, the dream can become a reality. How do you know if you have what it takes?

A 2003 study found the two most distinguishing characteristics of self-employed people were a strong work ethic and the inclination toward responsibility. Other factors such as education and family background were not nearly as significant. If you have the discipline to work hard and can take responsibility for your own success, you may have what it takes to go into business for yourself whether you're an introvert or an extrovert, young or old, experienced or amateur.

If you have mastered just a few techniques or have honed your skills for many years, you can create a viable market for your jewelry. From basic beaded necklaces to labor intensive cloisonné, buyers exist for every conceivable style and skill set. If you love to make jewelry, this book teaches you how to turn your passion into a thriving business. With the right information, hard work, and the willingness to take a chance, you will have everything you need to be successful.

Your Skill

Though you need a reasonable mastery over your work, your success will not be limited by your level of experience but rather your willingness to put yourself out there and take risks. Some of the most successful handmade jewelry designers employ only a few specific skills to produce the jewelry they sell. Consider Dillon Designs, for example. They sell beaded necklaces, bracelets, and earrings as well as a line of rings made from Shrinky Dinks.

Though the owner may be skilled in many areas of jewelry design, she employs just a few basics to produce the merchandise for her entire business. The beadwork and finishing details are excellent. The Shrinky Dink jewelry is beautiful. Because her work focuses on just a few skills, she has quickly perfected them and become quite successful in only two years. The Dillon Designs line sells in retail shops across the country.

If you have a great eye for beadwork, apply your talent to create a full line of products. If you've spent years mastering fabrication, design your pieces around the techniques you enjoy the most. When you focus on your strengths, you can perfect your skills and become an expert at your craft.

Quality of Work

If you're reading this book, chances are you've already received praise and support for your jewelry. However, if your work is poorly constructed or cheap looking, you need to improve your craft before you launch a business. Fortunately, classes are available in most major cities and towns where you can develop your skills fairly quickly. A few perfected pieces are all you need to inspire an entire line of jewelry.

The next time you visit a high end department store like Bloomingdales or Neiman Marcus, glance over the jewelry counter. You'll find a wide range of items—some that require incredible skill to produce and others that require very little. The complexity of a piece has little impact on its popularity. If a product is stylish, well made, and appropriately priced, people will buy it regardless of the skills or materials used to make it.

Your Style

Because buyers respond to a wide variety of tastes and styles, designers have carved out markets for jewelry made of everything from semi-precious stones to board game pieces. When you design new pieces, don't try to guess at what other people will like. Instead, focus on pieces that appeal to you. By creating something you like, you will simultaneously produce work that others appreciate as well.

Don't let yourself be intimidated by the abilities or creative talents of other designers. No matter how long you work in jewelry, you will always know people more talented than yourself. More significant than skill or experience is your unique approach to creating jewelry. Chapter 2 helps you create a style that suits you and your business.

Building Your Line

Though you won't need every article of jewelry (earrings, bracelets, necklaces) to develop a complete line, you will need a reasonable selection of pieces. Perhaps you have five or six pieces you know you can sell. How do you turn those items into a full line of jewelry?

Look to your existing pieces to inspire the rest of your products. You can use the same technique or application you've applied to previous items to create additional products or you can vary the shape and material of an existing piece to create spin-offs. If you've developed a signature item or element in your work, expand it into future pieces. Your items don't all need to look alike, but continuity in your line will help bring it together.

Inventory

Separate from your individual designs is your supply of finished pieces. Every piece in your line may be completely unique, or you may work from a set of designs that you re-create as they sell. Though your inventory will fluctuate as you produce and sell items, strive to keep your inventory high. Without products to sell, it's tough to make money.

If you have only five or six unique designs and zero replacement inventory, you can use the pieces you have to sell custom orders. Either re-create the pieces exactly, or take requests for slight changes to the original design (brass vs. silver, for example). This can be a great way to get some business while you're building your inventory.

To sell at trunk shows or fairs, you will need at least twenty or thirty designs and enough supply to replace items as they are purchased. Without sufficient inventory, pursuing these sales channels won't be worth the effort.

Preparing for Business

If you have no prior business experience, take comfort in knowing that most people who start a business have never done it before. Fortunately, the individual tasks are not difficult. By taking the initiative to read this book, you are already headed in the right direction.

Initially, all you need is a business license and your jewelry. Because a jewelry business doesn't require a large upfront financial investment, you can start as small and as slowly as you'd like. Your company will grow as you grow. Though you will make mistakes along the way, understand that some degree of trial and error plays a role in the success of every business venture.

You don't have to quit your job to learn the business and start selling jewelry. Unless you can support yourself financially, encourage you to start your business part-time. Chapter 7 presents several ways to sell your jewelry that can be implemented on a small or large scale. Once you can generate a sizeable and predictable income, you can decide when the time is right to transition to full-time.

Even if you have been making jewelry for years, a different approach and level of preparation will be required for business. The shift from hobby to career requires certain adjustments. Inspiration and creativity, though important, cannot be the sole forces to drive a successful business. In addition to designing jewelry, you will need to develop sales channels, attract customers, and handle administrative requirements.

This book teaches you to

- View your work from a business perspective
- Solidify your style and develop a niche
- Determine your target market
- Price your work
- Sell through a variety of sales channels
- Control costs and maximize profits

Starting a business requires three things: preparation, confidence, and a leap of faith. How do you know if it's right for you? The following chapters teach all you need to know about the business side of jewelry.

2

Style and Niche

As part of your jewelry, you will be selling a style and an image. When people buy jewelry, they also buy the feeling that the piece gives them when they wear it. Because jewelry purchases are based more often on wants than needs, your line, and the way it's presented, should create a sense of desire. You will achieve this through your style and niche.

The distinctive features of your line and the appearance of your displays will shape your style. Where you concentrate your creative efforts and define your place in the market will determine your niche. Together style and niche bring your work into focus and attract people to your products.

Define Your Style

When someone first notices your jewelry, what feelings do you want your pieces to evoke? Would you describe your work as boldly sophisticated, playful and whimsical, or something else? How you define your style determines how you present your business. From the typeface on your business cards to the materials in your display, style will influence everything.

If you don't already have a sense for the style your work reflects, identify a few descriptive and feeling words that capture what you're going for. See the examples on the next page for inspiration.

To form a clear style definition, first develop a list of three or four carefully chosen words that describe the look and feel you want for your brand. It's worth spending a few days to get it just right because you will use those words to inspire the outward appearance for all of your products, presentation materials, and displays.

For example, a style of jewelry described as "serene and understated" might use neutral colors and a minimalist display with price tags discreetly hidden. On the other hand, a charming and playful style might lean toward a more colorful presentation with non-traditional display furniture and hangtags.

Commit to your defined style and all of your decisions will be easier to make. Should you work with organic materials in the display or something more refined? Should you use bright, lively colors, or should you use tones that are more subdued? You'll find you can answer almost any question by referring back to your defined style.

Feeling Words

Confident	Unexpected	Happy
Joyful	Nurturing	Daring
Blissful	Amusing	Festive
Frisky	Playful	Lighthearted
Lively	Serene	Spirited
Tranquil	Empowered	Ethical
Powerful	Strong	Bold
Caring	Non-conforming	Calming
Passionate	Responsible	Secure
Love	Curious	Free
Peaceful	Unshackled	At Ease

Descriptive Words

Understated	Whimsical	Religious
Fun	Organic	Polished
Fancy	Creative	Casual
Classy	Conservative	Edgy
Funky	Modern	Classic
Antique	Costume	Dressy
Professional	Flashy	Sporty
Urban	Rebellious	Sparkly
High End	Sophisticated	Hip
Quality	Lively	Simple

Develop a Niche

A creative focus, also called a niche, will bring depth to your work and definition to your line. By concentrating you efforts on a niche, you will carve out a place for your business in the competitive jewelry market. Think of your niche as the role your business will play in the jewelry community. A niche will do several things to strengthen your business:

- It will attract customers
- Make you a specialist in your area of focus
- Make your work distinct and recognizable
- Increase the efficiency of your marketing efforts, materials purchases, and the use of your time

A niche will give you an edge over competition and improve your chances for lasting success. Do you have an area of focus, or do you need to create one? The next section outlines five ways to develop a niche.

Specialize in a Technique

Create a line of jewelry that centers on a specific technique or skill. If you enjoy fusing fine silver or have a knack for chain maille, for example, you can build your business around that technique. When a specific technique is applied to a line of jewelry, the line develops cohesion and uniformity based on the technique itself. This allows a designer more freedom to explore a wide range of jewelry styles without the pieces looking out of place within the line.

Consistent use of a particular skill increases your efficiency, reduces your labor, and over time, will make you an expert.

Concentrate on a Material

Many designers have created successful businesses using a few specific materials. The founder of Stonehouse Studio, for example, has created a popular line of jewelry using polymer clay and metal. This focus has led her to explore a variety of techniques and applications for the medium including the use of alcohol veneers and image transfers. With a few basic materials, she has developed an exquisite line of striking pieces. Jewelry from Stonehouse Studio is sold in boutiques across the country.

The exclusive use of just a few materials lends itself to discounted bulk purchases and can give jewelry a distinct and recognizable look.

Emphasize an Article of Jewelry

Make yourself known for resin pendants, wire wrapped bracelets, or natural stone earrings, for example. When you concentrate your efforts on a specific piece, you also concentrate your costs. Let's say your focus is natural stone earrings. Though you will use some peripheral supplies, the majority of your materials will be stones and earring hooks. Therefore, you can purchase these items in bulk quantities for lower costs and increased profit margins.

Additionally, emphasis on a specific item can make it easier for you to identify strong sales channels. For example, say you specialize in jeweled hair clips. The product may sell through the usual outlets but will also sell well in salons and beauty supply stores. It may even fit into boutiques that don't need additional jewelry lines but do need to diversify their merchandise.

Sell What Sells

Within your line and chosen niche, some items will naturally sell better than others. Your most accomplished piece, for example, may disappoint you when it's not a favorite among buyers. On the other hand, you may be surprised when an item you threw together at the last minute becomes a bestseller.

It can be difficult to predict the items people will buy and those they will disregard. Before removing pieces from your line, try different packaging, pricing, or a change in the display. If, despite your best efforts, nothing works, you need to discontinue items that don't sell well. Abandoning items that are less popular will make room for new, more profitable pieces in your line.

Alternatively, you should jump on your top selling items and pursue their full potential. When customers gravitate toward certain designs, materials, or themes, make more of them. You have complete control over the merchandise you offer, so it's up to you to provide more of what sells and less of what doesn't.

Focus on a Buyer

To create a buyer niche, target specific shoppers and provide products they will buy. For example, a woman I know in the Northwest sells jewelry every weekend at a Saturday market visited mainly by tourists. She sells gorgeous jewelry etched with orca whales and other local motifs. Her items sell for around $75 and make stunning keepsakes for tourists with money to spend.

When you concentrate your efforts on the buyer, it becomes easy to find customers. For example, the jewelry that sells so well in one Northwest town would probably sell well in other touristed cities within the region. To expand the business, she could approach tourist gift shops and hotels all over the Northwest.

Other buyer niches include jewelry for animal lovers, children, college students, new parents, sports enthusiasts, and world travelers.

Find a Theme

You may already have a passion that has led naturally to a theme in your work. Perhaps you design wedding jewelry or work primarily with healing crystals. Theme niches allow designers to directly target buyers and often open opportunities for sales in unconventional channels.

For instance, Wine Country Jewelry makes earrings, charm bracelets, and pendants designed around wine themes. They offer bead and crystal earrings shaped like grapes as well as a charm bracelet with charms in the shape of a wine glass, a bottle opener, and even a corkscrew. Wine Country Jewelry sells at over sixty boutiques and winery gift shops across the country.

Other popular jewelry themes include religion, animals, Celtic designs, holiday motifs, birthstones, astrology signs, and sports themes.

Trends and Fads

Even if your style is not considered trendy, trends will affect your business. While the latest fad lasts only a season or two, trends have staying power that can last for years.

- Trends influence the preference toward materials, colors, and size of jewelry.
- Don't be a slave to trends, but do pay attention to the styles and materials that are selling. Is larger or smaller jewelry more popular? Is gold outselling silver? Which direction is jewelry trending?
- Avoid fads. They often present as a craze (think Beanie Babies) and can become a costly way to sell jewelry when the fad changes before the inventory is sold.
- Be aware of when a style is on its way out. You will find greater success selling pieces with an up-to-date look.
- Browse celebrity magazines and those that target your demographic.
- Boutiques and high end department stores are reliable sources for jewelry trends.

Check Competitors - make a list of top selling items -

3

Know Your Customer

What products will you sell? Who will be your buyers? At first, the answers may seem obvious. You already know the type of jewelry you enjoy making and which pieces in your line have received the greatest praise. However, successful selling that can be sustained over time demands thoughtful answers that address trends, demographics, and your ability to meet customer needs.

For instance, your favorite pieces may not be your strongest sellers. The most time consuming pieces to construct may not sell for the price you need to justify that time. Trends in jewelry and fashion may dictate the direction of your designs. You may need to pursue alternative sales channels to reach your target market. How will you address these considerations before they become expensive problems?

To avoid mistakes, develop a marketing strategy *before* you begin selling. A marketing strategy will help you attract customers by first identifying their wants and needs. For example, does your customer want everyday jewelry or special occasion wear? Would s/he prefer to browse through the jewelry at street fairs or rather at boutiques? Will your customer buy a product that can't be returned? These questions and many more will help you indentify the characteristics of your target customer.

Your Target Customers

Can you describe the type of person most likely to buy your jewelry? Is your customer likely to be a man or a woman? An adult or a teenager? If your customer is a woman, how old is she? Where does she live? How much money does she make? Where does she like to shop?

Your first instinct may be to describe your target customer in broad terms that will include as many potential buyers as possible. Unfortunately, this approach gives you little information from which to form a marketing strategy. When you define your customers in specific terms, you can target them with specific strategies.

Corporations spend millions on customer research designed to produce effective advertising campaigns and to offer products customers will buy. Behind every ad or new product you see, are many hours of market research. You don't need a focus group or a consultant to be successful. However, you *do* need to think about your customers in a meaningful way based on definable characteristics.

Woman, aged 24 to 35, ideally shops high end stores, makes £30,000+, lives in high end areas - Montclair, NYC etc,

Research where this customer will be North Jersey bridal shows, salons & shops

Five F's of Understanding Your Customers

Function - Why will customers buy your jewelry? How does your product meet their needs or wants? What purpose does it serve for them?

Finances - How will a customer's overall financial position influence their jewelry purchases? How will the price of your jewelry affect a buyer's financial position?

Freedom - How and where do your customers prefer to shop? How easy have you made it for them to purchase products?

Feelings - How does your work affect or relate to your customer's self-image? How does your product make people feel?

Future - How will customers deal with your company in the future? Will they be inclined to buy from you again? How will you maintain the relationship?

This section will help you pinpoint details such as the purchasing patterns and buying sensitivities of your customers. Once you identify these and other specifics, you can tailor your business around them. For instance, perhaps your customer needs to feel like she's getting a deal and will respond well to special offers or promotions. Maybe she doesn't have time to shop and needs a way to buy your jewelry online. The more you know about your customers, the better you can serve them.

Next are five areas of market research that will help you understand your customer.

1. Demographics

Demographics describe characteristics of your target customer that include age, gender, income level, geographic location, and occupation. Once you've addressed the basic demographics, ask questions that are more specific. If you're unsure of an answer, do your best to make an educated guess.

- Are your customers likely to have children?
- Do they drive cars or use public transport?
- What is their level of education?
- Do they live downtown, near business districts, in the country, or the suburbs?
- Is the community diverse in ethnic and social backgrounds, or is it more homogenous?
- If your target customers are likely to be tourists, where are they coming from? What has drawn them to the area?

2. Lifestyle

Fortunately, jewelry contributes to every type of lifestyle on the planet. Because people make purchasing decisions that are specific to their lifestyles, it pays to understand the one you are trying to target. Here are a few questions to answer:

- What are your customers' interests?
- What kind of personal services do they pay for?
- How much money do they spend on image?
- How do you (or will you) relate to them?
- How do they spend their free time?
- What issues do they face in daily life?

3. Psychology

Psychographic descriptions attempt to explain *why* a customer makes a purchase. These answers enable you to focus on themes important to your buyer.

For example:

- Are your customers likely to be concerned about politics? Social causes? The environment?
- Is trend setting important to your customers?
- Are your customers driven by bargains?
- Is status important?
- Why do your target customers buy jewelry?
- On an individual level, how does she view herself?
- How does she want others to view her?

Once you determine the buying psychology of your customer, you can discern how to position your product-marketing. Should you mark your prices higher or offer more deals and bargains? Should you place emphasis on ideology or on expensive materials and exclusive pieces?

Catering to Customers

Once you define your customer, you can focus on a sales channel and product line that will draw in buyers. When you provide something specifically for them, customers will come to know your work and seek it out on their own. Your marketing will be most effective when you design your product, promotion, pricing, and overall shopping experience to appeal to your target customer.

4. Purchasing Patterns

You will create a favorable selling atmosphere and offer merchandise that customers are likely to purchase if you know how your customers like to shop, where they shop, and what they like to buy.

For example:

- Are your customers more motivated to buy personal items or to buy gifts for others?
- Do they shop often or just occasionally?
- Where do they like to buy jewelry?
- How much are they likely to spend on a single purchase?
- How long will they take to make buying decisions? A few days or a few minutes?

5. Buying Sensitivities

Depending on the customer, certain factors have greater influence on a buying decision than others. For some women, price plays a big role. For others, the acceptance of checks or credit cards can determine the sale. What are the buying sensitivities of your customer? Rank each of the items below as high, medium, or low sensitivity for your target customer.

- Price *Medium - low priority*
- * Quality *High priority*
- Promotions and discounts *Medium priority*
- * Packaging *High priority*
- Convenience of purchase *Low priority*
- Location of purchase *Low priority*
- * Presentation and display *High priority*
- * Credit cards accepted *High priority*
- * Customer service *High priority*
- Return or exchange policy *Medium priority*

* - focus on

Sample
Target Customer Description

Below is the target customer description for a Seattle based jewelry designer. It covers the five areas of marketing research: demographics, lifestyle, psychology, purchasing patterns, and buying sensitivities. Conclusions are drawn based on the information.

Demographics – Target customer is college educated, working woman, late twenties to early thirties. Still paying student loans but becoming more established in her career. May or may not be a homeowner. May or may not be married.

Conclusion – My target customer makes her own buying decisions and has some disposable income, but is not wealthy. My line will accommodate her stage of life by providing versatile, mid-priced pieces that she can wear both at work and at social engagements.

Lifestyle – She likely participates in the community and supports local artisans. Has many similar-aged and like-minded friends. Is socially active. Likes to be trendy, but not pretentious.

> Conclusion – The social network of my target customer makes her a great candidate to host home jewelry parties and open houses. Because word of mouth advertising is very effective in her social circle, I will strive to provide excellent customer relations and a positive shopping experience.

Psychology – Target customer is socially and environmentally responsible. Seeks individuality and a unique, but understated style. Persuaded by artistic integrity and value.

> Conclusion – I will place greater emphasis on individual pieces and work to bring a unique feel to my line. Marketing pieces and hangtags will tell the story of my business and reflect on my sources of inspiration.

Purchasing Patterns – She prefers to buy unique, quality-crafted, stylish pieces. Buys jewelry for herself more often than for gifts. Buys jewelry every two or three months.

Conclusion – My target customer is likely to be a repeat buyer. Business cards and a web presence will encourage and support future purchases. A mailing list to inform customers of new pieces and special promotions will also contribute.

Buying Sensitivities – Target customer will spend more money to get something unique. Often uses a credit card for purchases. Will want the opportunity to return or exchange. Influenced by presentation and packaging.

Conclusion – I will accept credit cards and offer an exchange policy – good for merchandise credit. I will use high-quality packaging materials and give attention to my product displays.

4

Professionalism

Your professionalism is just as important as your jewelry itself. The way people perceive your business will directly impact your sales and will largely determine your success. A reliable product, structured pricing, and reasonable policies are a few things customers expect from a retail transaction. Your business should meet those expectations and exceed them when possible.

When you present your business in a professional way, customers are more likely to make purchases and stores are more likely to consider your line. Professionals know what they're doing and are comfortable in their work environments. They always show up prepared. If you appear disorganized or unsure of your own policies, customers will question your ability to conduct business and will be less inclined to buy from you. A pleasant shopping experience and a smooth

25

transaction will keep the customer's focus where you want it—on your jewelry.

Attitude

If you don't have a lot of confidence with customers, you will have to fake it until you do. Confidence tells customers that you can be trusted and that your work is made with integrity. Trust is what allows customers to move forward with a purchase. It rarely develops without some display of confidence from the designer.

Some people naturally exude confidence; most of us have to work at it. There are three universal ways to appear confident, even when you're not:

1. Smile and make eye contact
2. Offer a friendly but firm handshake
3. Stand and sit with good posture

Appearance

Dress appropriately for the venue. If you are at a street fair, for example, a cocktail dress will look out of place. On the other hand, if you present pieces at a charity gala, leave your Birkenstocks behind. When you expect to be on your feet all day, wear comfortable shoes. When you're in front of potential customers, always wear your jewelry. When you meet with boutique owners, it's appropriate (but not required) to dress according to the style of the store.

Like it or not, people will judge your appearance. Don't go out of your way to be someone you're not, but be aware of how your personal look reflects on your work. You make a stronger impression when you present yourself professionally.

Business Name and Image

With few exceptions, customers expect to make purchases from businesses rather than from individuals. Choose a name for your business that is simple and easy to remember. Avoid generic names like "Stacie's Jewelry Design". Instead, choose descriptive words that are meaningful to you or your work. Look for inspiration in the real life examples below.

Jewelry Business Names

Gem and JewelryWorks	Sequin
Links of London	Rock a Bead
Bead Candy	Silver Cherry
Baubles n Things	Metal Art
Simply Silver	Pearlworks
Leaves of Glass	Flying Anvil
Pieces of Me	

Contact Information

You will need a phone number and email address where people can easily reach you. A dedicated phone number, like a cell phone or separate business line, is more professional than one shared with other people. Change your voice mail from a casual greeting to a professional one.

Your business email account should be separate from your personal email address. You can obtain a free account from Hotmail, Yahoo, Gmail, and many others. If possible, find a way to incorporate your business name, or part of it, into the email address.

Business Cards

You can order a box of business cards for around $20, or you can print them on cardstock and cut them yourself.

Business cards should include your name, business name, phone number, and email address. If you have a website or other information, such as stores where your jewelry can be purchased, it should be listed as well.

You will give your card to customers, boutique owners, and other contacts you make in the industry. A standard business card is two inches tall and three and a half inches wide.

Sample Business Card

The Modern Pearl
Stacie Vander Pol

Phone	712-555-3535
Email	ModernPearl@gmail.com
Website	www.TheModernPearl.com

Aim to:
Get a new #
phone #
with message

Order Forms / Invoices

Use invoices or receipts that produce duplicate copies. You can retain one for your records and give the other to your customer. You can purchase receipt pads at office supply stores for a few dollars. For custom orders, be sure to include the customer's name and contact information (for future contact and marketing opportunities) on the invoice in addition to descriptions and prices of the items.

If you don't want to list your home address on public documents such as these, you can obtain a PO box address from your post office or substitute the mailing address with a web address. You can purchase a custom ink stamp or print labels from your computer to place in the company information section.

Sample Invoice

Invoice #26058

Company: Date:

Address:

City, State:

Phone:

Quantity   Item Description   Price

Subtotal:

Tax:

Total Due:

The Modern Pearl

Stacie Vander Pol

www.TheModernPearl.com

TheModernPearl@Gmail.com

712-555-3535

Wholesale Price Sheet

Product	Item Number	Whls Price	Retail Price
Large Silver Hoops	3021	$12	$24
Small Silver Hoops	3020	$9	$18
Large Brass Hoops	2021	$16	$32
Small Brass Hoops	2020	$12	$24
Five Strand Bracelet	1501	$34	$68
Single Strand Bracelet	1500	$12	$24
Five Strand Necklace	1401	$75	$150
Single Strand Necklace	1400	$28	$56

Minimum First Order $150

Additional Orders $50

All Sales Final

Orders Ship In Five Business Days

Payment Terms: Net 15

Need to do this & work out pricing correctly for each piece.

Once I have this list, then approach bridal salons with press pack.

Double!

SELL YOUR JEWELRY

Price Sheet

A price sheet, also called a line sheet, is necessary for selling your jewelry in retail outlets such as gift stores or boutiques. Professional price sheets contain complete contact information, company policies, and two sets of prices (wholesale and retail). The wholesale price is what you will charge the store. The retail price is the recommended selling price, commonly known as the MSRP.

As your business progresses, you may want a more sophisticated price sheet that includes photographs of each piece and volume discounts for large orders.

Professional Policies

Before you begin selling, you should be clear about your policies. Customers will need to know which forms of payment you accept, where you stand on returns and exchanges, and how custom orders will be handled. Established policies give you a professional appearance and ensure your customers are treated fairly and respectfully.

Your policies should be clear and firm. That doesn't mean you can't change something that isn't working. It just means you shouldn't offer different policies to different customers based on a whim or impulse. Know where you stand on all of your policies *before* a sales event or presentation. You have several to consider.

Accepted Forms of Payment

Cash and checks are the most common ways to accept payment. As your business grows, you will likely expand your payment options. Additional forms of payment encourage purchases and increase sales.

Cash – If you plan to accept cash, be sure you always have plenty of coins and small bills available to make change. Cash is safe and easy to accept but it can limit your sales. Most people will bring $40 to $60 to a jewelry sale only to find later that they don't have enough cash for everything they want to buy.

Checks – When you accept a check, make sure the address on the check matches the one on the driver's license, the dollar amount is correct, and the check has been signed. If you have a checking account in your business name, it is okay for people to write checks to your business. Otherwise, they will need to make checks out to your name.

Credit Cards – If you go directly through a bank or credit card company, you will be charged 5% of the sale price plus a monthly fee and an initial set up fee. You can expect to pay around $300 in fees each year plus 5% of every sale.

Alternatively, for around $79 a year, you can use a company like ProPay.com to process credit cards over the internet or the telephone. This is a suitable option for open houses and home parties. You can call in the payment information or enter it on the web. Fees are approximately $0.35 plus 3.25% of the final sale price. A $60 sale, for example, will cost you $2.30 in fees. To sign up or learn more, go to ProPay.com.

PayPal – Anyone who has made an online purchase is familiar with PayPal. This payment alternative allows customers to buy goods through an online account with a credit card, debit card, or checking account. PayPal

SELL YOUR JEWELRY

does not charge a monthly fee or set up fee. The transaction charge is $0.30 plus 3% of the dollar amount. A $60 sale will cost you $2.10 in PayPal charges.

PayPal is an option when a computer and internet access are available. To collect money, the customer can log in, click the Send Money tab, and enter your email address with the dollar amount. Alternatively, you can request money from a customer from your own account. Your customer will receive an email with instructions on how to pay. For more information, go to PayPal.com.

Return Policy

Sales environments such as trunk shows and craft fairs, which last only a day or two, can make returns a logistical impossibility. It's okay to vary your return policy depending on the sales channel. And it's okay not to offer a return policy at all.

If you offer a return policy, make the terms clear on either the invoice or a sign. The policy should have a time-frame (thirty days from the purchase date, for instance). It should also clarify if the return will be for merchandise credit or cash back. Returned merchandise should be in new and unworn condition.

A reasonable compromise is to accept returns within a two week period from the initial purchase for merchandise exchange only. This will encourage people to buy gifts they might otherwise be unsure of because the recipients can exchange the items for something else.

Guarantee

Though it is not common for small jewelry designers to offer guarantees, eventually someone will ask about your policy. It's better to know where you stand ahead of time than to be put on the spot. Decide your policy *before* you are asked.

If you decide to offer a guarantee, be specific about what it includes. If a customer snags their beaded bracelet and rips it apart, for instance, will you replace it? If a stone pops out of its setting, will you repair it, replace it, or refund the money? Does normal wear and tear qualify? If not, where do you draw the line?

Guarantees can be tricky. Use your own judgment (and comfort level) to determine how you will handle broken, bent, or failed pieces.

Store Orders

Boutiques and other retail outlets will expect you to have clear policies that are specific to wholesale orders. Most designers require retailers to spend a minimum amount for the initial order. This ensures a fair representation of the line and makes certain the owner is serious about selling it (and not just looking for a discount on a few personal pieces). A safe place to start is $150 (at wholesale prices) for the initial order and little or no minimum for subsequent orders.

$150 Minimum opening order

Custom Orders — *Introduce a design fee $30 (x2 sketches)*

$50 Minimum thereafter

Many successful designers sell custom orders exclusively. They advertise through word of mouth and occasionally sample their pieces at offices and other workplace settings to encourage orders. For other designers, custom orders are a side business rather than the main source of sales. If you decide to accept custom orders, you should have established policies in place designed specifically for this type of sale.

For example, I recommend you request payment upfront to cover your cost and prevent buyers from backing out once you've already begun the work. Avoid the temptation to ask

SELL YOUR JEWELRY

customers how or when they would like to pay. Such an approach comes across as unprofessional rather than considerate. Instead, let them know your policy.

If the order is for a unique piece that the customer has yet to see, it may be reasonable to require 50% down with the balance due upon completion. Let customers know how long it will take to complete the item and how it will be delivered. Be sure to collect contact information in case you have further questions or require last minute alterations to the piece.

[handwritten: Non Refund-able]

[handwritten: Develop a bespoke order page on AJB website (- more simplier)]

Professional Presentation

The way you present your jewelry sets the tone of your work and informs people of its quality. Attention to detail in packaging and display can mark the difference between a professional and an amateur. Chapter 6 covers all you need to know about display and presentation.

Packaging

Your packaging doesn't have to be elaborate, but it should be consistent and streamlined. Even if you're just selling at a friend's house, don't bring a hodge-podge of sacks and bags to package sales. To foster positive word of mouth advertising, which will generate future sales, show up prepared with proper materials.

You should have a system for packaging each piece of jewelry you sell. Perhaps you wrap earring cards in small cellophane bags and you place necklaces in gift boxes. Packaging is an area where a little creativity can go a long way.

Display

[handwritten: - Think about display for bridal shows (Vintage inspired)]

Your display will set the stage for the overall look and feel of your jewelry. In fact, the way you display your work can say more about your line than the product itself.

Depending on how they are presented, you could sell the same two pairs of earrings and ask very different prices. A pair of earrings, for example, will sell for a higher price when presented with thoughtful display and presentation than it will tossed in a bin with twenty other pairs.

Price Tags — *Tiny price tags for parties + shows*

The prices of your items should be easy to find and read. People don't like to ask how much things cost. Ensure the shopping experience is relaxed and pleasant by including a price tag or visible sign for every piece of jewelry.

Promotions and Deals

Make a plan of sales times in the year (special promos for Valentines etc)

I encourage you to offer special sales and promotions as long as they are not excessive. Too many promotions will confuse customers and appear unprofessional. Special deals can spur sales, but you should offer no more than one or two at a time.

Promotions are most effective when they are clearly stated or visibly advertised. How many times have you walked into a store, shopped around, chosen an item to buy, and then found out at the cash register that your item is 20% off? It's great for you, but it didn't do the store much good if you were willing to buy it at full price.

Promotions are designed to encourage sales. However, they only work if people know about them. If you offer a two for one special, for example, make it known before customers make their buying decisions.

5

Pricing

How you price your work will have a direct impact on sales as well as profit. Overpriced jewelry will give you a high return—often at the expense of sales. Underpriced merchandise may generate more sales but will cut into your earnings. How do know which price is right?

Appropriate pricing is competitive with products of similar style or quality and does not compromise profit. Several factors can influence the price of a product:

- Cost of materials
- Cost of your time *charge $20 p/hour.*
- Overhead costs
- Market value of the item
- Profit
- Desirable price point

Cost of Materials

At a minimum, pricing must cover the cost of materials. When it doesn't, your business is costing you money. The cost of your materials includes everything you use to make an item excluding tools and machinery. The price of every bead, clasp, piece of solder, wire, and other materials should be included in this category.

Cost of Your Time

What is your time worth? Your time must be worth something or you wouldn't have started a business. Decide how much you want to earn per hour. I suggest between $20 and $30 an hour to start. Most designers start low and increase their pay as they become more efficient and established.

Depending on the method for price calculation, the cost of your time usually refers to the time you spend to construct and assemble your pieces.

Overhead Costs

Your overhead will depend on the type of jewelry you make and the techniques you employ. Overhead includes the cost of equipment, workspace rent, office supplies, postage, invitations, advertising, travel, and packaging materials. A website, the cost of fairs or shows, and the cost to list items online are also overhead costs.

Market Value of the Item

Market value has nothing to do with your skill level or the quality of your materials. Market value is the actual price people will pay for an item or service. To estimate the market value of an item, shop your competition to find out how much people pay for similar jewelry. For an accurate estimate, look at successful lines with strong sales.

How to Pay Yourself

Owning a business might be the American dream, but it can become a personal nightmare if you don't make it a priority to pay yourself. Consider your own salary one of the many financial obligations of your business. You wouldn't think of stiffing a supplier. Treat yourself with the same respect.

You can pay yourself by writing checks out of your business checking account (see page 93) on a regular basis or after each sales event.

Before you start your business, decide how much money you want to make. This will help ensure that you pay yourself. It will also help you set goals and stay focused on the business side of your jewelry.

Profit

After you subtract the expenses (materials, time, and overhead) from your income, the money left over is your profit. Because profit is calculated *after* you pay yourself, you can invest it back into your business with new tools, employees, equipment, or education. You also have the option to pay yourself a bonus. *Invest profit into the business- more flyers, business cards, advertising, shows. etc*

Desirable Price Point

When you design a new piece of jewelry for your line, you should have a target price point in mind. Say, for example, you are designing a new bracelet. If other bracelets in your line cost between $45 and $75, you should aim for a price point somewhere in that range. On the other hand, if you are trying to attract budget conscious buyers with the new item, your price point should be lower.

A pre-determined target price will help you choose materials and fabrication methods that coincide with your price point. If an item falls outside your desired price range, look for ways to cut costs. You can look for lower cost materials or change the design to bring labor costs down. This will ensure you do not end up with a product that your target customer can't afford or is unwilling to pay for.

Determine the Price

This section describes three ways to calculate retail and wholesale prices. The retail price is what you charge for any sale made directly to a customer. This includes sales through trunk shows, flea markets, and the internet. If you sell your jewelry at shops and boutiques, those retailers will pay you a wholesale price (usually half of the retail price) and sell your items for the retail price.

You can use multiple pricing methods simultaneously on different pieces within your line, or you can stick to a single method that works best for your business.

Double Time and Materials

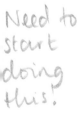

The most common way to determine the wholesale price is to double the cost of time and materials. You can double the number again to arrive at the retail price.

For example, say it takes you fifteen minutes to make a necklace that costs you $4.00 in materials. If you pay yourself $20 an hour, your labor cost on the piece will be $5.00. When you combine a $4.00 materials cost with a $5.00 labor cost, you get $9.00. When you double that number, you get a wholesale price of $18.00 and a retail price of $36.00.

This formula is simple to use and easy to calculate. However, it does have limitations. For example, a simple pair of wire earrings that cost a couple of dollars and a few minutes to make could probably sell for more than this pricing strategy would suggest. On the other hand, an item that takes hours to produce may have to be priced lower than this method's calculations because the time cost could drive the price prohibitively high.

More Time and Materials

This approach is similar to the previous one but places greater value on your time. In this case, your hourly wage includes:

- Design time
- Time to shop for materials
- Construction and fabrication of the item
- Time to sell the piece

To calculate the wholesale price, combine your hourly wage for all of the steps named above. Then add the cost of materials. Double that number for the retail price.

Say, for example, you spend $120 and one hour shopping online for supplies to make 20 necklaces. If it takes you 10 hours to make the necklaces (half an hour each) and three hours at a home party to sell them, your total time for the necklaces, from the design to the sale, is 14 hours.

Twenty dollars an hour salary multiplied by 14 hours gives you $280 for time. Add $280 to $120 (materials cost) to arrive at $400 for total time and materials. Divide $400 by 20 necklaces to get a wholesale price of $20 per necklace and a retail price of $40.

This method can be cumbersome because you need to track your time so closely. However, it ensures you are paid for *all* of your time. This formula is most suitable for designers with a consistent and predictable sales channel (like home parties or Saturday markets).

Cost of Materials

To calculate the wholesale price with this method, you will triple or quadruple the cost of your materials. For example, a bracelet that cost $7 in beads, findings, and wire would wholesale between $21 and $28. Double that number for the retail price. Avoid this method for pieces made of very high or low cost materials. It will skew those prices either too high or too low.

Though this formula is simple to calculate, I hesitate to recommend it to new designers because it does not examine how much time you spend on construction. If you don't track your time, you will never know what your time is worth (or if it's worth your time).

Increase the Value of your Jewelry

Do you know the difference between a sterling silver bracelet sold at Tiffany for $450 and one sold at a craft fair for $75? The answer – perceived value. Though the bracelets may be very similar, customers perceive one to be of greater value than the other and therefore expect to pay a higher price.

If the workmanship is of the same caliber and the materials are identical, why can one command a higher price than the other? The answer can be found in the product's ability to satisfy *other* customer needs. This section describes four ways to add value to your jewelry and command higher prices by appealing to a customer's *perception* of value.

Higher Prices

[handwritten: Beautiful packaging, well written, professional emails. 10% off card, whole package presentation. Create an upscale feeling]

Higher prices on their own can increase the perceived value of products. Take wine, for instance. In a recent study, researchers at Stanford Business School found that price had more influence than taste had over the perceived quality of wine. The subjects, who were told only the price of each wine, rated a $45 bottle much higher than a $5 bottle of the same Cabernet and a $90 bottle much higher than its $10 twin.

In settings like this one, customers place a higher value on items that cost more, even when the price is the only evidence presented to support their perception. In this case, higher priced wine tastes better. In the jewelry market, higher prices work well for custom made jewelry as well as target customers who seek out and are willing to pay for exclusive pieces. Examine your target customer description (Chap. 3) to determine if higher prices will positively influence your buyers.

Consistent Quality

Products that hold up over time develop a reputation for quality. Consider All-Clad kitchenware or Snap-on tools, for example. You know when you buy an All-Clad pan, it will last for years, if not decades. Even though the pans cost twice as much as the competition, All-Clad can justify the price because their pans do not wear out. The same goes for Snap-on tools: They can charge more because the quality of their products is worth the price.

A reputation for quality doesn't develop overnight, but once your products become known for quality and durability, you can charge significantly more for them.

Expensive Materials

Even minor additions of high end material to your jewelry can increase your selling price. The addition of materials like fresh water pearls or venetian glass can allow you to increase the price far more than the added cost of the material. And even the smallest amount of diamond or gold can double the retail value of an item.

Tiered Pricing

Offering a range of prices can increase sales. Low priced items sell well for impulse purchases, and a few high end items can increase the value of your entire line.

Develop a few pieces that are inexpensive and easy to make. Sell them at a lower price than the rest of your line. They will appeal to those buyers who can't commit to a high priced item but who have been inspired to buy something.

Because some shoppers will only be interested in your best work, create a few high end pieces from materials or applications that are more expensive. Tiered pricing will expand your appeal to a wider range of customers and bring diversity to your line.

For example, a friend of mine sells a line of sunglasses which retail for around $90. When a few, small Swarovski crystals are added to the side arms, the price jumps to $130. The crystals cost only a few cents each, but customers perceive them to be more valuable. Enough so, that they will pay significantly more for them.

These materials won't increase your sales if you are the only one who knows about them. In fact, they will only increase your costs. If you add fresh water pearls or 14-karat gold leaf, for instance, promote it on a sign or tag and make it a strong selling point.

Presentation

The *way* a product is presented can be the biggest factor in the price. Consider restaurants, for example. Let's say a deli charges $6.50 for the soup and salad combo served to go in Styrofoam containers. The friendly staff includes plastic utensils and paper napkins in a lunch sack for you to carry home.

How much more could the restaurant charge for the same soup and salad if it were served on plates at a cozy table dressed in white linens with a romantic candle centerpiece? $12.50? $15.50? The food may be the same, but the appealing presentation and improved dining experience justify a higher price.

The next chapter teaches you to present your jewelry in way that both attracts customers and supports your price.

6

Presentation

The only thing more important than the quality of your work is the way it is presented. A high end display increases the perceived value of jewelry; poor presentation reduces it. Because merchandising and display have so much influence over the value of products, the way you present your jewelry directly affects your sales.

A display and presentation that reflects your style and speaks to your target customer will pay for itself many times over. Your display is often the first thing to attract customers to your work and can influence whether or not a purchase is made. This chapter outlines what you need to create a distinct presentation.

Packaging

Packaging includes earring cards, descriptive tags, tissue paper, boxes, and bags. Your packaging materials should fit within your style and work together in color and theme. It's easy to overspend in this area, so pay close attention to cost. With some thought and a little effort, you can develop simple packaging concepts that look good and save money too.

Bags and Boxes - Simple bags or boxes usually work better than more elaborate packaging, as long as they are consistent with your overall style. Add embellishments such as tissue paper, ribbons, stickers, or other finishers to create a custom feel. You can rubber-stamp your logo on any of these items as an inexpensive way to build your brand.

Earring Cards and Other Packaging - You can save money and customize your packaging when you make it yourself. For example, you can iron artistic paper to felt or cardstock with Perma-Bond fusing adhesive, found at fabric and craft stores, to create custom earring cards. Use a tiny hole punch to form the holes for earring posts and wires. Alternatively, you can order a wide range of packaging materials from outlets like Rio Grande or from online sites such as retailpackaging.com.

Display Materials

Materials include the fixtures from which you display your jewelry to the colors and materials that adorn the table. Avoid loud or busy background prints that distract attention away from your jewelry. Display materials should do three things: strengthen your look and feel, contribute to your defined style, and enhance your work rather than compete with it.

Trays, bowls, and plates found at yard sales and thrift stores can hold most types of jewelry. To vary the look, drape fabric over trays or fill bowls with tumbled glass, crushed rock, sand, or stones. You can purchase these items at home and garden stores or craft shops. You can wrap shoeboxes in paper, fabric, or other medium, and then turn them upside down to serve as inexpensive pedestals.

You can purchase display furniture, including earring stands and bracelet bars, through jewelry wholesalers and retailers. I recently saw large jewelry stands at Claire's Boutique (an inexpensive jewelry store found in many malls). You may find you have to assemble some of your own pieces to get it just right. Don't hesitate to add spray paint or other decorative effects to improve the color or finish.

Create Your Display

The way you show your work should set the mood for your jewelry and attract your target customers. You can create a display in five steps:

1. **Stick to your style.** Your display will set the stage for your jewelry (literally) and should reflect your desired outward appearance. Let your defined style be your inspiration and a guide for your choices. As you choose materials and colors, ask yourself if they contribute to the style of your work.

2. **Limit your color choices.** If your style definition includes certain colors, use them in your display. Cool blues and blacks enhance the look of silver pieces. Warm colors, like deep reds and chocolate browns, are great for showing off gold and brass. As a rule, limit your colors to two or three. Too many become more of a distraction than a contribution.

3. **Consider set-up.** An elaborate display might appeal to you until you realize it takes over an hour to set it up and another hour to take it down. You will need to adapt your display for different selling environments. Consider how difficult or easy it will be to set up your display each time and how often you'll have to replace (or clean up) display materials such as sand, rocks, or flowers, for example.

4. **Create depth.** When every piece of jewelry is placed on a level tabletop, the items tend to blend into one another and appear ordinary. Varied levels and heights of merchandise add dimension to your display and distinction to your pieces.

5. **Let it shine.** Jewelry always looks better with good lighting. At shows and fairs, bring your own spotlights and extension cords to highlight your work. Just be sure the light shines on your jewelry and not into the eyes of potential customers. At open houses and home parties, try to set up your display in a well lit area of the house. If necessary, don't hesitate to bring your own lighting.

Descriptive Tags

You can attach hangtags to your items that offer a description of the piece itself or tell the story of your jewelry line. Some tags state the name of the item and list the materials. Others offer background about the designer, the inspiration, or the process of making the piece.

Like other components of your presentation, the way your products are described should be consistent with your defined style and should appeal to your target customer. Is your target customer more likely to be interested in the inspiration behind the design or the expensive materials used to create it?

To find the words you're looking for, reflect on your pieces. Identify details, such as a material or finish, that make your items special or unique from other jewelry. For example, say you work with a line of multi-strand beaded necklaces comprised of sterling silver, quartz, and Czech glass beads. These distinct materials should form the descriptions of your work.

If your focus is a specific technique, use creative language to describe it. For example, say your signature pieces have a sandblasted finish or roughed up surface. Whether you describe it as sandblasted or storm finished, make sure the description conveys something unique about the piece.

Recycled Materials

Depending on your demographic, you may or may not want to advertise the use of recycled items in your work. Some customers will naturally place higher value on such pieces, but don't assume that everyone will. Just because you choose to be thoughtful about recycling doesn't necessarily mean it will help your sales. For some demographics, it may even hurt sales. Though it is commendable to re-use materials, consider how your target buyer will respond. Some people will always prefer "new".

Effective Promotional Words

The following list provides just a few of the everyday materials and techniques that can create effective promotional words and phrases:

- Handmade
- Hand crafted
- Artisan crafted
- Oxidized
- Antique
- Antique finish
- Copper, brass, silver, gold, steel, iron, gold filled
- Blown glass
- Recycled or reclaimed
- Crystals (use the name of the crystal)
- Any natural gemstone (use the name)
- Swarovski crystal
- Fresh water pearls
- Czech glass
- Lampwork beads
- Venetian glass
- Millefiori beads
- Vintage
- Fused (glass or silver)

One Product Five Ways

The examples in the next section illustrate how the same pair of earrings can be positioned to fit five different styles (exotic, urban, earthy, whimsical, and sophisticated) and reach different target customers. The earrings in each example are made of simple beach glass wrapped in sterling silver wire. Note how different product descriptions, prices, and presentations paint a unique picture for each one.

Sterling Silver and Saltwater Glass

Product Presentation - Earring cards made with bamboo printed paper fused to cardstock.

Display - Wood bowls half filled with red lava rock, on brightly colored fabric, interwoven with silk scarves. Alternatively, wood planks could be used (available at flooring stores) instead of bowls.

Colors - Bright red, oranges, blues, and very dark brown.

Packaging - Wrapped in a single color tissue paper and placed in a small, brightly colored fabric bag, pulled closed with a ribbon (found a craft and packaging stores).

Price - $35.00

Price Tags - Curvy handwriting on bright cardstock.

Hangtag – "Collected from coastlines around the world".

Ocean Glass in Silver Wire

Product Presentation - Earring cards made of thin, grey rubber sheets cut to size.

Display - Earring cards rest in a bed of washed pea gravel (available at home and garden stores).

Colors - Dark, charcoal grey with small accents of bright orange, red, or green.

Price - $24.00

Price Tags - Typed sticker on the back of the earring cards.

Packaging - Wrapped in a solid color tissue paper then packaged in a clear cellophane bag, folded and sealed with a company logo sticker.

Hangtag - Ocean glass wrapped in sterling silver wire.

lia sophia®

You may purchase the Flapper Necklace for only $10!

With a minimum $600 Show in February

Free-spirited fringy fashion reminiscent of the 1920s for spontaneous fun all day (or all night)! A burst of brilliant clear cut crystals, tasseled hematite chain and genuine hematite beads. Have a roaring good time!

As a Hostess with a Qualified Show, you are entitled to:

FREE Jewelry
Receive 20% of your Show sales in **free** jewelry credits to be used on regular-priced items.

Hostess Bonus Items
Purchase up to four items of your choice at the special Hostess Bonus price of $15 each (unless otherwise stated).

HALF-Price Items
Purchase up to two items of your choice at HALF price.

40% Hostess Credit
Have 10 orders and two dated bookings from your Show and get 40% of your Show sales in jewelry credit for only $15. To be used on regular-priced items.

(91H22)

Join Us. Getting Started is **Easy!**

Substitutions may occur.

$149

You'll receive a Starter Kit filled with jewelry and all the business materials you'll need to get your business started with success.

February 2011 **New Advisor Special**

Submit a minimum $600 Starter Show, receive a $100 Jewelry Premium!

Jewelry Premiums are great for adding styles to your kit!

Jewelry **$100** Premium lia sophia®

Sue Peterson

Call me: 732-754-8719 (cell)

Email me: susanapeterson@aol.com

Visit my website: www.liasophia.com/susanpeterson

Recycled Beach Glass Hand Wrapped in Silver

Product Presentation - Earring cards made of stiff felt. (You can buy it at fabric and craft stores).

Display - Earring cards displayed in clear glass bowls filled with beach sand.

Colors - Muted greens, rust, and soft browns.

Packaging - In a corrugated cardboard gift box tied with a piece of any color raffia.

Price - $18.00

Price Tags - Simple, handwritten prices on white tags attached with white string (you can buy these by the hundreds at office supply stores).

Marketing Words - Natural, recycled, reclaimed, artisan crafted, sterling silver, handmade.

Polished Glass in Silver Baskets

Product Presentation - Dangling loose from a wire clothes-hanger or a screen.

Display - Fabric draped over a table with various sized sea shells adorning it.

Colors - Soft plums, pinks, and silver.

Packaging - Wrapped in tissue, placed in a small bag, and tied with a curly ribbon.

Price - $29

Price Tags - Playful font on medium sized tags.

Marketing Words - Collected, handmade, beach glass, wire-wrapped.

Satin Sea Glass in Sterling

Product Presentation – Loose pairs, without earring cards.

Display – Black or grey stones large enough to comfortably display a pair of earrings.

Colors – Black and silver with a touch of dark blue or purple.

Packaging – White or single color tissue paper with matte black or glossy white gift boxes.

Price – $45.00

Price Tags – Small black tags handwritten in silver pen, attached with string.

Marketing Words – Solid sterling silver, uniquely selected glass stones, individually hand crafted.

7

Making the Sale (Part 1)

Jewelry is so popular in our culture—it can be sold almost anywhere. Even small salons and spas will carry a line of jewelry from a local designer because they know it will sell. Depending on your ability and willingness to travel, the number of outlets for jewelry sales is virtually unlimited. Exploring just one of the many options can produce enough sales to support a small business.

Open houses, office parties, and online sales will help you gain experience and build confidence. These sales channels are relatively inexpensive and require less commitment and preparation than other venues demand. Once you become proficient and comfortable with one of these channels, you can focus on it exclusively or use it as a launching pad to expand into other sales venues.

This chapter walks you through the process of selling through four entry level sales channels.

Open House

The informal and fun gathering of an open house, where the shopping is relaxed and the time is constrained to a couple of hours, is a nice way to make several sales in an afternoon. The best part - you don't have to leave your house. Open houses require little upfront time and money, making them a great place to test the waters.

Invite over a group of friends, neighbors, or co-workers to drop by for food and drinks as well as an exhibit of your jewelry. People can come for a few minutes or a couple of hours—whatever suits them. Because these get-togethers are mostly social, it's easy for people to show up. Guests will expect to enjoy themselves while looking over your pieces. If you offer a range of prices, you can usually sell at least one item to every person who drops by.

Use these step-by-step guidelines to host an open house.

Step 1

Decide on a date and time. Then make a list of people you wish to invite. If you have several groups of friends or colleagues, you can invite them all or host multiple parties. Create an invitation for an afternoon of food, fun, and jewelry. Discreetly explain the forms of payment you will accept so people can come prepared. Request an RSVP one week before the event.

Step 2

Send out invitations three weeks prior to the party. Prepare a menu and plan for tasteful decorations. Let skeptical friends know they don't have to buy anything, but if they see something they like (and they probably will) it's okay to purchase it.

Sample Invitation

An afternoon of wine, cheese, and
Lots of fun jewelry await you
at
My House, 132 E Main St.
on
Saturday, May 15th

Stop by anytime between 2pm-4pm.

Feel free to bring a friend
RSVP by May 7st at 206-555-6358

Cash and Checks accepted for jewelry purchases.

Step 3

Set up a professional presentation of your jewelry. Make sure each piece is clearly marked with a price tag or visible sign. Place your items in a central location of the room. They will show best if you can vary the height within the display. Set out several mirrors for people to use when they try things on.

Decide on a promotional deal to offer as a sales incentive. For example, "receive 15% off your purchase when you spend over $100". Or, "receive a free pair of earrings for every $50 you spend". Remember to limit your promotions to one or two, and know that it's okay not to offer a promotion at all.

Set out food and beverages as well as any decorations.

Step 4

Greet people as they arrive, take their coats, and offer them something to drink. Thank people for coming and introduce them to other guests. Provide information on your pieces. If you use a special technique or material, for example, mention it. You don't need to explain every detail—just enough so people realize your pieces are unique.

Step 5

Assist people with clasps on necklaces and bracelets. Encourage everyone to touch and try on your jewelry. As you circulate through the room, show people different ways to wear the pieces. If you have a promotion, remind people of it.

Step 6

Write up invoices and package items as they are purchased. Remember to include a business card and thank each person for stopping by.

If you run out of inventory on a piece, suggest a similar alternative or offer to make the piece by way of special order. For special orders, the customer pays for the item and receives it when you complete it.

Open houses are a great way to test the popularity of new pieces and get feedback on your line. Host an open house as often as you want. Plan for a big one (with plenty of inventory) in the weeks leading up to the holidays.

Sample Party Menu

Appetizers

Cheese & crackers

Fruit platter

Chips and dip

Beverages

Wine

Sparkling water

Soda

Ice

Decorations / Other

Flowers in vases

Music

Dessert

Cupcakes

Candy & nuts

Serving Pieces

Trays and utensils

Plates

Napkins

Wine glasses

Water glasses

Home Parties

If you like selling in your home but don't know enough people to host an open house every weekend, you can ask friends to host parties for you. Most women are familiar with Tupperware, candle, and ornament parties, which are hosted in someone's home, with her own invited friends.

A jewelry party at a friend's house works a lot like an open house, with a few exceptions. Your friend will usually handle the invitations, provide the refreshments, and invite a group of new people to see your jewelry. For home parties, use the open house guidelines with the following changes:

- Once you've selected a friend to host a party, set a date and time. Either you or your friend can send the invitations. However, if you do it, emphasize on the invitation that your friend will host the party.
- Arrive one hour early to set up your display. Remember to lay out several mirrors. You won't need to provide food and drinks—the host will do that for you.
- Instead of people streaming through, the party will begin and end just as the invitation states, so everyone will arrive at the same time. After the guests settle in, thank them all for coming, introduce yourself, and give some background on your pieces.

- Start the party by compensating the host with a piece of jewelry. Remind the group that they too can receive free jewelry when they host parties.

- Work the party just like you would for one in your home. Enclose a business card with every purchase. At the end, thank everyone, especially the host.

SELL YOUR JEWELRY

The key to success with home parties is to have the confidence to ask people to host them. Supportive friends and family members are usually willing to help by throwing at least one party a year. To expand your base, ask those outside your inner circle - loyal customers are the best places to start.

Workplace Sales

If you work in an office environment or know someone who does, you have an opportunity to sell jewelry. Office sales are favorable because the right offices can generate a lot of business with little effort on your part.

Follow these steps for selling in the workplace:

Step 1

Ask friends and family, who support your business, to bring a sampling of your jewelry to work. You can offer an incentive—say 20% of sales or a free piece of jewelry, though you might be surprised how many people will be happy to help for no compensation at all.

Step 2

Use a decorative tray or cover a box with fabric that compliments your defined style. This will serve as your travelling display.

Step 3

Decide if you want to sell your pieces outright or if you want to send samples. If you sell the pieces outright, consider sending multiples of each piece. If you plan to take orders from samples, create an order form that includes a space for the customer name, contact info, item name, item number, and cost.

Four Ways to Pay Thanks

Success often involves the help and support of key people along the way. Whether it's for a jewelry party or an introduction to a boutique, you have several ways to thank those who help you:

1. A piece of jewelry of his/her choosing
If you're in an office setting or home party, let the recipient choose the jewelry for everyone to see. This will get people in the shopping mood and encourage others to host in the future.

2. A piece of jewelry you pick out
A bracelet or a pair of earrings, for example.

3. A gift certificate for your jewelry
If the gift is for a party host, present it at the party.

4. Pay a percentage of sales
Tally up the total spent and pay your host in cash or merchandise credit, based on a percentage of sales you previously agreed upon.

Step 4

Gather the pieces you wish to send. Label each one with a price tag and an item number. Using the item number, record the items you send.

Step 5

Send the display and order form with your friend to his or her workplace. Your friend will show your jewelry to co-workers. They will buy items either by filling out the form or by purchasing directly.

Step 6

Your friend will collect payments and return to you the unsold jewelry along with payments and order forms. You will then pay the compensation you both agreed on.

Step 7

Fulfill the orders, include a business card, and label each package by customer name. Either you or your friend can deliver the items to the workplace.

Once you discover the locations where your jewelry sells well, send a box of new items every month or two.

Expanding Your Opportunities

Need help brainstorming for sources of home or office sales? Try this guaranteed exercise. First, take out a sheet of notebook paper and number it one through 100. You can make two columns and use the back of the page if you need more room. Once you are finished numbering, begin making a list of all the people you know.

Like most people new to this exercise, you're first thought will probably be, "I don't even know 100 people, let alone know them well enough to sell my jewelry to them." Start writing anyway. The names don't have to be good leads, just people that you know. Once you think of twenty names, you can usually think of five more. Then another five. Then another. Don't stop until you've filled in all 100 slots.

I have used this method hundreds of times for sales training classes, and it has never failed to work. You just have to be committed to filling in all of the spaces, even if many of the names will not be useful leads.

The first names will come easily, friends, family, and co-workers. After the initial steam wears off, and you find yourself stumped, use the following list to trigger more names.

Who are your...?
Extended family members
In-laws / cousins
Nelghbors
Co-workers
Hairdressers
PTA members
Dentists / doctors
Former co-workers

If you still haven't reached the magic number, look in your cell phone and in your email address book. If you don't reach 100 names, answer these questions:

Who do you know that...?
Is a newlywed
Is a new mom
Is always busy
Works in a salon
Works in an office
Works for a large company
Works for a non-profit

Works in a medical office
Works at a law firm
Works too much
Works part time
Is a nurse
Is a swing shift worker
Is a small business owner
Is a working mom
Is a stay at home mom
Is going back to school
Is a student
Works for a start-up company

Once you have filled in 100 names, go back and put a star next to the best leads and a check mark next to the second tier leads. If this list generates at least twenty possible leads, you're in business. Now, all you need is to contact each person with a special request. Offer some form of compensation (a pair of earrings or a percentage of sales, for instance) in exchange for hosting a party or bringing your jewelry to the women of his/her workplace.

When pursued consistently, this strategy can generate enough business from home and office parties to keep you busy full time.

Online Sales at Etsy.com

Launched in 2005, Etsy began as a small website where just a few hundred people from all over the world bought and sold handmade merchandise. Today, Etsy sells half a million items a month for an annual sales revenue of more than $84 million.

While most jewelry designers don't do the bulk of their business through Etsy, a few have made it a primary source of income. Whatever your goals, Etsy is a great way to establish a professional online presence for little cost. Anyone can set up a storefront through Etsy with no set up cost or monthly fees.

Etsy sellers have virtual storefronts complete with personalized web addresses: www.username.etsy.com. You can include your Etsy web address on business cards to point existing customers and potential retail accounts to other items in your line. User friendly and inexpensive, Etsy charges $0.20 for each listed item. Items remain on the site for four months or until they are sold.

Tips for Success on Etsy

1. **Use high quality photos of your work**— preferably with a plain background and excellent lighting. You can hire a professional, though many successful Etsy sellers have learned to take their own photographs. For more on jewelry photography, read *Ebay Photos that Sell*, by Dan Gookin or *Taking Great Pictures for eBay Auctions and Online Selling*, by Rod March.

2. **Provide detailed descriptions.** Etsy shoppers like to know what they are buying, so be sure to offer generous descriptions of your work including the dimensions, size, materials, and the technique.

3. **List a substantial inventory of products.** The top jewelry sellers on Etsy have 100 to 200 items listed at any given time. More items for sale increase the chance that people shopping your store will see something they like.

4. **Provide company background information.** Etsy allows users to write a bit about themselves, their companies, as well as their policies. A complete profile page and structured policies lend a professional and established appearance to a virtual storefront.

5. **List items that can sell in the $5 to $40 range.** The best selling Etsy stores price most of their jewelry under $25. Though this price point is low for handmade jewelry, designers have learned how to make money on Etsy. The secret is to keep costs down and sales high. Green Thumb Designs, for example, has created a low cost line using buttons and other found objects that are fastened to inexpensive silver plated ring bands and hair clips. At $5.00 to $10.00 an item, they price their products to sell. Estimates show Green Thumb at over 7000 sales and $175,000 in revenue since 2007.

6. **Have a niche.** This was covered in Chapter 2 but is worth repeating. Every successful jewelry designer on Etsy has a niche. Take Madison Craft Studio, for example. They sell nothing but pendants made from origami paper. In the past two years, they've sold over 9000 pendants and grossed more than $45,000 in sales on Etsy alone. In another example, Gemma Factrix sells jewelry made from sterling wire and

jump rings. In less than three years, her Etsy store has sold over 4000 items, for approximate revenue of $180,000.

7. **Keep your prices low and your costs even lower.** Eighty percent of the purchases made on Etsy total less than $40.00. To sell so inexpensively, designers have to keep their materials cost low and their production time down. You will have greater success on Etsy with items that are easy and inexpensive to create.

8. **List often.** Because Etsy posts newly listed items on their main page every 15 seconds, you can increase your exposure by listing a few items each day rather than listing everything at once. If you have duplicates of an item to sell, list them individually as opposed to marking the item as "multiples available." The extra effort will increase your exposure on the home page and won't cost a dime.

8

Making the Sale (Part 2)

Part two of Making the Sale looks at outlets that require more commitment and preparation than those covered in part one. Success with craft shows, street fairs, and retail outlets demands greater professionalism and organization. In exchange for your effort, these venues expose your work to a much larger audience than you could find on your own. If you are willing to spend some money upfront and do some legwork, the channels covered in this chapter will reward you with higher income and increased sales.

Any one of the sales channels in this book can be exclusively pursued to develop a successful business or combined to create a comprehensive sales strategy. Focus on sales outlets that appeal to you the most. You will find greater success when you pursue work you enjoy.

Markets, Street Fairs, and Craft Shows

College campus fairs, street fairs, Saturday markets, farmer's markets, and craft shows can generate enough in sales to earn a full time living. The average flea market receives over half a million visitors each year. Even if only 10% of those people see your booth, that's 50,000 customers! With over 10,000 venues to choose from, the opportunity is enormous.

Research

The most important thing you can do to ensure your success at fairs and shows is to find the fit. At a minimum, your research should uncover three things: the cost of the show, the number of attendants expected, and the number booths accepted. If you have the opportunity, check out the show before you commit to a booth. Unfortunately, it is quite common for new designers to waste money and time at shows that don't generate enough sales to cover the cost. You can avoid this mistake.

If you research thoroughly, you will turn down more opportunities than you accept. Quality far outweighs quantity. The best shows are those that see many visitors who fit the profile of your target customer. The research takes time. However, once you find the right fit, you will be rewarded with steady and predictable sales.

A Google search will help you find listings of the fairs and markets in your area. The searches suggested below will give you the information you need, including dates and descriptions. Type the name of your city and the words...

- schedule of street fairs
- schedule of farmers markets
- schedule of festivals

When I type "Seattle schedule of street fairs" into Google, for example, the first listing is a Seattle.gov page that lists over sixty different fairs and festivals that take place in the Seattle area. Some happen once a week, others only once a year. I can click on each one and be taken to a webpage devoted to that specific fair. See the websites listed below to find the fairs, markets, and shows in a particular state or region.

Online Resources

www.MagicYellow.com/category/Flea_Markets/Cities

www.GreatFleaMarket.com

www.States.FarmersMarket.com

www.IndieCraftShows.com

Your Booth

As visitors stroll through a fair or show, the first thing they see, before they even notice your jewelry, is your booth. Because the draw of your booth itself is so important, it's okay to spend some money for an eye catching display.

Rely on your defined style or niche to inspire your ideas. It's easy to let enthusiasm take over. Just don't let your booth overtake your jewelry. If your jewelry looks crowded on the table, customers will have a hard time discerning individual pieces and will be less inclined to purchase something. Place jewelry in groupings so that you can leave some open space in the display.

Packing List for the Show
- Plenty of mirrors
- A pad of invoices and a handful of pens
- A calculator to tally sales and calculate tax
- Good lighting to enhance your display
- Water and discreet snacks you can eat quickly
- Business cards
- If you accept cash, bring plenty of coins and small bills so you can provide change
- An emergency bag of tape, scissors, ribbon, twine, a Sharpie marker, and construction paper (for quick fixes and impromptu signs or packaging)
- A table cover and chairs (if necessary)
- Your jewelry and display furniture

Show Day
Your booth will be more attractive and inviting if you stay on your feet and smile at everyone who approaches. Though it's okay to take breaks once in awhile, you will be more successful by appearing active at your booth.

Encourage shoppers to try on your jewelry. Assist them with clasps and fasteners. Be quick with a mirror and a genuine complement on how the piece looks on them. Explain the materials or techniques you have used in your work and why your pieces are unique.

If you're at an all day fair or show, bring a lunch with you. When you find it's time to stop for a snack, sit toward the back of the booth, yet close enough to keep an eye on your inventory. Never eat in front of customers or while a customer is visiting your booth. That being said, make sure to eat lunch. You will regret it if you don't.

SELL YOUR JEWELRY

Evaluation

Calculate the revenue generated after every show and fair. Then subtract the cost for the booth space and any money you spent to prepare for the show. Look at how much you're left with and determine if the money you made was worth the time you spent. Success with booth sales is a process of elimination based on trial and error. With proper venue research and commitment to a great booth, you will develop a list of profitable shows that contribute to the growth of your business.

Boutiques and other Retail Outlets

Boutiques can include high end pet stores to specialty food stores and everything in between. Fortunately, most all of them sell jewelry, even if it's just a small display at the front counter. Small retail shops are always looking for new products that will appeal to their customers and are grateful when they find them.

The next section will prepare you to work successfully with boutiques and small retail outlets.

Pricing

Provide storeowners with a price sheet that outlines both the wholesale and retail pricing of your line. The recommended retail price of your jewelry should be the same at all sales outlets including boutiques, online, home parties, and shows. See Chapter 5 for pricing information.

Minimums

Boutiques will expect you to have required minimums, at least for the initial purchase. $150 is a good place to start for the initial order. Because all serious designers have minimums, wavering on this policy will lead stores to doubt your experience. I encourage you to set firm policies and stick to them. See page 34 for more on minimums.

Terms of Payment

Be clear about how and when you expect to be paid. Payment for the first order is usually due on or before delivery of the merchandise. You can ask for cash on delivery for the first purchase and net 15 or net 30 (payment is due 15 or 30 days after items are received) for future orders.

Retail Outlets to Approach

Art galleries	Tourist gift shops
Day spas	Yoga studios
Country clubs	Museum stores
Resorts	Bridal shops
Nail salons	Hair salons
Clothing boutiques	Gift shops
College campuses	Coffee shops
Christmas stores	Shoe stores
Hospital gift stores	New age stores
Hotel gift shops	Retirement centers
Pet shops	Religious bookstores

Returns

You will not be expected to accept returns from stores for merchandise that did not sell. However, if it helps you get the sale, offer a return policy for the first few months while a store works your line into their offerings. If you decide to make this exception, inform the storeowner that you are making a special exception for them and will accept returns only for a defined period.

Check In

Check in on your local accounts at least once every month or two. This will give you a chance to replenish inventory and to see how your jewelry is merchandised within the store. If something doesn't look right, suggest an alternative. Store visits will also help build relationships with storeowners and open opportunities for future sales.

How to Re-order

Let storeowners know the best way to place additional orders. Should they call, email, or visit a website? Will you stop by to take orders in person?

Turn Around Time

Let the buyer know how soon he or she can expect to receive your products once an order has been placed. Don't promise faster service than you can deliver. It's better to set realistic expectations now than to deal with an unhappy shop owner later.

Research

Compile a list of boutiques that are potentially good targets. Once you've found a few stores that might be interested in your jewelry, ask for the owner or manager's card so you can call back to schedule an appointment. Most shop owners have time slots each week or month set aside to meet with designers and view new merchandise.

Make Appointments

When you're ready for an in store presentation, call the shop to make an appointment. Ask to speak with the appropriate person (manager, owner, or buyer), introduce yourself, and explain the purpose of your call. Use the following phone approach as a guideline.

"Hi, my name is _____. I am a local jewelry designer and I was in your shop the other day. The reason I'm calling is I thought my jewelry might (pick one from below)
  a.   be a good fit in your store
  b.   compliment your other merchandise well
  c.   appeal to your customers
and I was hoping to stop by real quick to show you a few pieces in my line. Does that sound okay?"

Interested storeowners will book an appointment with you. If they aren't interested at that time, ask if it would be okay to check back in a couple of months. If so, be sure to call back at that time. Polite persistence is the key to scheduling appointments.

The Appointment

Dress professionally and wear your jewelry. Remember, the boutique's customers always come first, so don't be frazzled if your meeting is interrupted. Wait politely and pick up where you left off. Come prepared with a smile and the following materials:
  • Price sheet with wholesale and suggested retail prices
  • Examples of your work in a portable display case
  • Calculator and pen
  • Order sheets or book of receipts

- Business cards
- Pictures of your jewelry (if you have them) either on postcards, brochures, or a laptop

Follow Up

Send a thank-you note for follow up. Keep a log or record that includes contact information and notes for each store you visit. If you didn't make the sale on the first attempt, don't be at all discouraged. Just be sure to follow up and foster the relationship. Eventually, your efforts will pay off.

Trunk Shows

Unlike the name implies, trunk shows do not take place out of the back of a car but rather anywhere a designer can show up with a "trunk" of merchandise to sell. Usually a one day affair, trunk shows are a low cost, low commitment way to generate sales. When successful, they benefit all the parties involved.

Before they agree to carry your line, some boutiques will allow you to do a trunk show. This allows them to see how their customers respond to your designs before they commit to a wholesale purchase. If things go well, you stand to gain a new account. In other cases, trunk shows allow you to sell your work at outlets that wouldn't normally be inclined to carry jewelry. A trunk show at a coffee shop or salon, for example, can make for a great afternoon of sales. The storeowner benefits from the increased traffic and attention, while you get the opportunity to expose your work to a new audience with no overhead costs or admission fees.

Trunk Show Tips

1. Approach salons, spas, boutiques, card stores, gift shops, and coffee shops with a sample of your jewelry and suggest a trunk show.

2. If the owner does not expect to share revenue - great. You can pay thanks with a piece of jewelry. Otherwise, agree on a percentage of sales *before* the show. Never pay a storeowner more than 50% of your sales revenue.

3. Create a professional and appealing display that will attract customers to your table.

4. When working a trunk show, smile and greet people who approach the store. If your jewelry is well displayed, customers will naturally come over to take a look.

5. Show up prepared with everything you might need. See page 78 for a supply list.

6. Thank and compensate the owner.

7. If the show goes well, suggest another one.

You will be responsible for setting up your table and creating the display (either outside the door or somewhere inside the store). The store will be responsible for promotion. You can help by notifying your email list and customer base and by providing the store with flyers that announce the upcoming show.

In most cases, storeowners will expect to receive 50% of the sales revenue generated from a trunk show. However, if you're a patron of a particular shop or have a relationship with the owner, you may be allowed to host a trunk show without sharing the profits. In this case, you should find another way to thank them. Free jewelry works well.

Consignment

Before they commit to new merchandise, some stores want to test the product and see how it sells without forking over the upfront costs to bring in a new line. One way to meet the needs of these storeowners is to consign (or lend) your jewelry to the store at no cost. If the items sell, the store will pay you a percentage of the revenue.

Consignment allows stores to build their inventories for no cost, and it allows unknown designers a way to present their products to the public. Though consignment is less popular than other sales channels, it can be one of the best ways to get your foot in the door of retailers, especially when you're starting out.

If your jewelry sells well on consignment, the store will be more inclined to purchase future merchandise at wholesale cost. Other stores that have a "consignment only" policy will continue to stock your items and pay you the agreed percentage. If your line does not sell well, keep looking. You will eventually find a good fit that will reward your efforts.

Expect to receive between 60% and 70% of the sale price of your jewelry. However eager you may be to get your product into stores, be wary of those who offer you only 50% commission. Avoid those who offer anything less. Remember, the store risks nothing to stock your items while you, on the other hand, give up inventory with no compensation until it sells.

Because you will give up your inventory without being paid, make sure the store is a good fit for your product. Check to see that the shop is busy with plenty of customers from your target market. Don't waste your time (and merchandise) on stores that don't see strong sales. Your inventory will be better suited in another sales channel than it will collecting dust on the shelves of a slow consignment shop.

Any time you consign your jewelry, sign a written agreement that outlines the following expectations:

- The exact percentage you will be paid and any additional fees that will be charged
- How and when you will be paid
- A timetable
- Who will be held responsible for lost or stolen merchandise
- How and when you can retrieve unsold items
- How the store will display your products

Successful consignment requires good record keeping. If a store fails to record the sale of an item properly, you may return to find your jewelry is gone and the store has no record of the sale. Without a record, the store will not pay you. Instead, the owner will insist that you must be mistaken, that the item you're referring to was never in the store to begin with. You can avoid this predicament with a little research.

Before handing over your work for consignment, ask how sales are tracked and recorded. If you don't feel comfortable with their system, move on. You can request monthly or quarterly transaction reports to track how well your items perform. Work to expand your presence in high performing stores. Pull your merchandise from stores that don't generate sales.

9

Your Business

Setting up a business is easier than most people realize. You need little more than to complete a few administrative tasks, most of which can be done from your computer in a couple of hours. Online, you can obtain a business license, a sales tax number, and business checking account. Once completed, these steps will make you official.

Running that business successfully, however, is a much greater challenge. Success in business requires ongoing dedication and a willingness to change course when things aren't working. The path your business takes will depend on your goals and your commitment to seeing them realized. Success is up to you. Thoughtful planning and preparation, *before* you begin, will make the task of operating your business easier.

This chapter provides you with the steps you need to establish a company as well as the strategies you need to position it for success.

Business Structure

To establish your business legally, you must first choose a business structure. Options range from cheap and easy to costly and complicated. If you are unsure of the best structure for your needs and goals, talk to a lawyer or accountant.

Sole Proprietorship – This is the simplest business structure and the easiest to set up. A sole proprietorship is owned by one person. That person owns all of the profits (or debts) generated by the business. Income from the business is taxed as personal income and is reported on a personal tax return to the IRS.

As a sole proprietor, you can create a DBA (Doing Business As) to conduct business under a name other than your personal name. Sole proprietorship is the most common business structure in America and is the choice for most designers.

General Partnership - A partnership works like a sole proprietorship but is owned by two or more people. As with a sole proprietorship, the partners own the profits and the debts. Each partner reports his or her earnings or losses on individual personal tax returns.

If you chose to partner with someone, the specifics of your agreement should be defined in a signed contract. Specifics include:
- How profits are to be distributed between partners

- How much money or other capital each partner has contributed to the business
- Each partners' rights and responsibilities
- How a partner can leave the business
- How the assets will be divided if both partners agree to terminate the business

Limited Liability Company (LLC) – LLCs can be owned by one person or by multiple partners. Unlike the structures previously described, owners of an LLC are not personally responsible for the debts and liabilities of the company. Therefore, if the business is forced into bankruptcy, debtors cannot come after an owner's personal finances to pay the debts.

Like the above mentioned structures, LLC owners report their profits or losses on personal income tax returns. As with a general partnership, a written agreement should be formed between partners.

LLCs are charged with initial set up fees, filing fees, and annual state fees, which are all more expensive than the cost of a sole proprietorship or general partnership.

Business License
Easy and inexpensive to obtain, your business license will make you official. Type into Google (or other search engine) the name of your city and the words "business license". You will quickly find the site you need. Most of the time, you can fill out the information right on the website or print out the forms from your computer.

Your business license needs to be renewed annually. Each year you will receive a bill in the mail from your city government to pay for the renewal. Fees for a business license range from $0 to $150, depending on where you live.

Sales Tax Number

If your city or state charges sales tax for purchases, you will need to register with your local Department of Revenue Sales Tax Division. This can be done at the same website where you obtain your business license. Once registered, you will receive a resale tax number, which you will use to pay sales tax. A sales tax number will also allow you to buy wholesale supplies and materials without paying sales tax.

Sales Tax

Depending on your state and city regulations, you will be required to collect sales tax on each sale. Here's how sales tax works: You will charge customers a tax based on the amount of the sale, and then you will pass the payment on to your local government agency.

You can find the percentage to be collected on the sale of goods at your state and city government websites. Sales tax is based on the dollar amount of the sale (not including shipping) and is charged based on where the sale takes place. Online or mail order items are taxed based on the city where the product is shipped.

When you complete a sale, add a line on each invoice for the sales tax. Be sure to keep your copy of all invoices so you have a written record. Each quarter, you will receive a form to send back with any sales tax you owe to your state's Department of Revenue.

If you participate in shows or fairs in other states, be sure to follow the sales tax requirements (they differ by state). In some cases, you can obtain a short-term tax permit; others require a standard permit.

Employer Identification Number (EIN)

Even if you don't plan to have employees, wholesalers often require an employer identification number (EIN) as proof of your business status. Once you have employees, you will use the EIN to report and pay employee tax. If you don't receive an EIN with your business license, you can request one for free from the IRS at IRS.gov.

Bank Account

To keep business and personal finances separate, open a checking account for business transactions. If you set up an account under the name of your company, customers can write checks (if you choose to accept them) out to your

Mailing Address

If you don't have a separate studio address, it's fine to open a bank account and acquire a business license using your home address. However, I don't recommend listing it on other publicly viewable sources like a website or business card unless you plan to operate a retail outlet out of your home. If you seek a more professional appearance, but don't have a separate business location, you can sign up for a post office box at USPS or a postal service shop like The UPS Store.

company name instead of to you. To open a business account, the bank will ask to see your business license and EIN number.

The bank will issue a checkbook in your company name and may offer you a credit card as well. I find a separate credit card especially helpful for tracking my business related expenses. If I put everything I buy for business purposes on the company credit card, I don't have to sort through the line items of my personal credit card statement to separate my business purchases from the others.

Accounting

Small business accounting is easy to maintain. You shouldn't have to hire an outside bookkeeper, though you can if you want to. Either way, you need to keep records of your expenses and your income. You can use a software program such as Quicken or a much simpler, but equally effective, system of two shoeboxes. One box will store your receipts for purchases; the other will hold your copy of invoices for sales. At the end of the year, you'll sort them out, total them up, and ta-da—your accounting will be done.

Workspace

If you work from home, you'll need a dedicated workspace that can be easily isolated from pets and children. Though your work area will vary according to the type of jewelry you make, all functional work stations should include the following:

- Storage area for completed pieces
- Storage for findings, materials, and packaging
- Storage for receipts and invoices
- Good lighting
- A height appropriate work station
- Supportive seating

- Shelf space for instructional or inspirational books and magazines

If appropriate, add ventilation, a utility sink, a computer, and a dedicated area for the use of power tools and torches.

Start-up Costs

Starting a jewelry business can be as costly or affordable as you want. Determine how much money you need to start your business by calculating your start-up costs. The list below contains common costs for starting a jewelry business. Line items will vary depending on the type of jewelry you plan to sell and the tools or supplies you already own.

Start-Up Cost Checklist

		Cost
Facilities and Fees	Rent for studio space	
	Membership to use studios	
	Deposits for rentals	
	Business license	
	Upfront cost for shows and fairs	
Equipment	Furniture	
	Tumblers	
	Polishers	
	Casting machines	
	Kilns	
	Compressors	
	Rotary tools	
	Computers / Software / Printers	
	Camera for photographing work	
	Telephone	
	Storage furniture	
	File cabinet	
Office Supplies	Receipt book	
	Business cards	
	Brochure printing	
	Paper for invitations	
	Pens	
	Bookkeeping software	
Materials	Raw metals	
	Wire	
	Beads	

		Cost
Materials	Enamel	
Cont.	Stones and gems	
	Findings	
	Displays	
	Packaging materials	
Tools	Torches	
	Soldering supplies	
	Pliers	
	Drill bits	
	Saws	
	Adhesives	
	Hammers	
	Abrasives	
	Liver of sulfur	
	Wax and carving tools	
	Files	
	Tweezers	
Education	Classes	
	Workshops	
	Books	
	Subscriptions	
Other Costs	Website design	
	Accountants or consultants	
	Marketing fees	
	Advertising	
	Promotion	

Business Goals

Getting what you want isn't always easy and the path to success isn't always clear. As a business owner, you will be the driving force behind your own success. Even if you don't consider yourself goal oriented, I encourage you to define what you want from your business. Without knowing where you want to go, how will you know when you're heading in the right direction?

To address these questions, business owners set goals. Goals provide entrepreneurs with the guidance and motivation they need to excel. Goals help us form a plan and give us a way to evaluate our performance. In short, goals help us succeed.

Outline Your Vision

What kind of business do you want to run? Do you envision a small business where you wear all the hats, or would you prefer to work with a hired staff? Which sales channels will you start with? What are your long-term goals for sales outlets? You don't necessarily need to know how your business will look in five years, but if you know what you want to achieve, it will be easier to make decisions as you progress. You can establish a plan of action once you have a clear vision.

How much income do you want to earn? When starting out, set different tiers of financial goals. For example, during first six months of your business, your financial goals should be more conservative than they will be after two years. Once you decide how much you want to earn, you can work back from there to determine how much you need to sell.

When and how often do you want to work? Do you want to work part-time or full-time? Are you open to working weekends? Nights? It's important to set some boundaries.

Without them, you can find yourself working too many hours and compromising other areas of your life.

Set Goals

The next step is to establish concrete goals that are both meaningful and measurable. There are four steps to setting a goal.

1. Define a Specific Goal and Write it Down

A goal must be well defined to serve as an effective business tool. The more specific the goal, the easier it will be to achieve. A generic goal like, "I want to succeed" is not specific enough to formulate a plan. Instead, set your goal based on something concrete such as a dollar amount of revenue or a number of items sold.

Once you have the concepts in your mind, it's important you write them down. Studies show that people are far more likely to achieve their goals when they write them down. You can post them in a visible location or tuck them away for later review. Either way works, as long as you write them down.

2. Break Large Goals into Smaller Goals

Let's say your goal is to make $2000 a month. To achieve this goal, first break it down into specifics. How many pieces do you need to sell to earn that much revenue? How much inventory will you need to ensure the number of sales? How many sales events will you need to attend to meet your goal?

The best way to reach a large goal is to set attainable short term goals you can measure. Use these examples to get started:

- Commit to increase your inventory to a certain level.
- Approach a specific number of acquaintances about jewelry parties and workplace sales.
- Commit to create a certain number of new designs each quarter.
- Commit to a certain number of sales events each month (trunk shows, parties, fairs).
- Approach a specific number of boutiques each month (if this is part of your larger goal).

3. Set Deadlines

Deadlines are important for three reasons: They force us to create schedules and hold ourselves accountable, and they give us a way to measure progress. On occasion, you may need to modify your deadlines. Unforeseeable events in life and in business can set your timeline back or speed it up. When circumstances influence the scope or timeline of your goals, adjustment them.

For example, you may meet someone who is able to help you get your jewelry into stores much sooner than you expected. In this case, you need to go back and change both your deadlines and your goal itself. On the other hand, an event in your life that delays your progress may dictate that you set your timeline back.

4. Work from a Plan

Once you have written down the specifics of your goal, broken it down into smaller goals, and set deadlines, it will be easy to form a plan. Use a calendar or spreadsheet to write down the tasks for each week. When you don't complete your day's assignments, simply move them to later in the week. When you just can't bring yourself to work on a task designated for the day, pick one from tomorrow's list. As long as you do something each day that moves you forward, you will eventually reach your goal.

Grow Your Business

Once you outline your immediate goals, consider your long term plans. Ask yourself the questions below, scratch down some answers, and revisit the list every few months.

- Where do you see your business in five years? Will you have more employees? Which channel will be your primary source of sales? What products will you be selling?

- Do you want to eventually expand your sales channels? If so, what are they and what is your timeline?

- Do you want to diversify your products? Will additional training will be required to expand your product line? Define it. Will you need to acquire additional equipment?

- Will you need new skills to achieve your long term goals? What is your plan for ongoing education and instruction?

Form Strategic Alliances

One way to grow your business is to partner with a related company. Collaboration works best when the outcomes are mutually beneficial and both parties have something valuable to offer. For instance, a company with a large customer base and a firm with a large production facility could form a partnership to benefit them both. By joining forces, the first company gains access to the production equipment while the second gains access to new potential customers.

Keep your mind open for opportunities to collaborate with other people in the jewelry industry. Consider these possibilities:

- Partner with established and successful designers to learn from their experience.
- Work with designers in fields that don't directly compete with you.
- To decrease costs and lighten the workload, team up to share a booth at shows.
- Collaborate for bulk buying power on wholesale purchases.
- Work out trades—say raw or finished materials in exchange for photography services or graphic design.
- Collaborate with a designer who has skills you lack and offer a trade.

10

Lower Costs
and Higher Profits

Popular products and a large volume of sales can sustain a business only when those sales generate profit. Profit is what you will use to invest in new equipment, expand your skills through training, and grow your business. Profit is the reason people go into business and is what separates businesses from charities.

You can grow your profit without raising prices or selling more merchandise. Though you should always strive to do both, there is another solution. When you reduce the time required for fabrication and lower the cost of your materials, your profit margin will automatically increase. This can mean more money in your pocket or investment in your business. In addition to increased margins are other benefits. By reducing fabrication time, you can produce more product. By lowering costs, you can be more flexible with pricing. Bottom line: Your company profits when costs are controlled.

See the difference in profit before and after costs are cut in the example below.

Cost and Profit for 20 Necklaces

Before Cutting Time and Material Costs
Cost of Materials - $100
Cost of Time - $30 x 5 hours = $150
Total Costs - $100 + $150 = $250
Wholesale Price - 2 x $250 = $500
Your Profit - $500 - $250 = $250

After Reducing Costs
Say you cut the cost of your time and your materials by 20%, but maintain the same wholesale pricing.

Cost of Materials - $80
Cost of Time - $30 x 4 hours = $120
Total Costs - $80 + $120 = $200
Wholesale Price (unchanged) - $500
Your Profit - $500 - $200 = $300

Cost of Time

How long does it take you to produce a single item? How long does it take to produce ten items? At $20 or $30 an hour, your time is worth money. If it takes only twice as long to make ten items as it does to make one, you know that you should always construct the item in multiple quantities.

Because you can produce only so much in one day, you will either work within the boundaries of this limitation or find ways to increase capacity. This section covers the four most common ways to save time.

Casting

Casting is the process of creating metal pieces or components from a mold. Professional casting companies cast items in gold, silver, platinum, pewter, brass, bronze, and other metals. After you pay a small set up cost, most items can be cast for less than a dollar and smaller components for just a few cents.

If you have a metal component or completed piece you repeatedly create, have it cast in bulk quantity instead of making each one by hand. The price of casting is very reasonable considering how much it can save you. Say, for example, you have crafted a pendant from metal clay. Ounce for ounce, you know that metal clay costs more than sterling silver. You know the time it takes to form the pendant and the time and energy costs required to run your kiln. At what point does it make sense to cast the item you create so often from clay? It is probably sooner than you think.

To have an item cast, send in the piece you need replicated to a professional casting company (see the list on page 136). The casting service will first build a mold for the item. They will then pour liquid metal into the mold to recreate the piece, with a total turn around time of less than a week. You will receive lower prices with volume orders, but you can order a single copy if that's all you need.

Purchase Finished Pieces

It's okay not to design every single component of your jewelry yourself. You can buy pre-manufactured findings to save time or to fill in gaps where you don't have the skills.

For example, say you have been successful with a line of beaded necklaces that hold your signature fused silver pendants. How would your business improve if you could buy the necklace pre-made then embellish it with your own touches and your own pendant? The cost of materials would probably increase but your time would decrease.

Successful jewelry designers know how to supplement their own jewelry with pre-fabricated pieces, which they either embellish or sell as-is. Many jewelry suppliers and wholesalers offer a selection of pre-manufactured pieces. Here are a few time saving items:

- Stone settings
- Ring bands
- Ear wires
- Simple necklaces
- Clasps
- Cuff bracelets

Hired Help

You have several options for hired help. Unless you are prepared to take on an employee, pay employee tax, social security tax, and possibly offer employee benefits, I recommend you start by hiring independent contractors instead of employees. Independent contractors are responsible for their own taxes and benefits. You can pay them a straight wage without additional expenses or paperwork.

106   *SELL YOUR JEWELRY*

They can be paid by the hour, by the day, or by the job. If you can't monitor how efficiently your contractor is working, you can pay based on the number of completed pieces. This will make your time cost easier to calculate for each item and will ensure you get what you pay for.

Equipment Purchases

Is there a tool or piece of equipment that would speed your production time? How long would it take to pay off the cost of a new equipment purchase? Proper tools and equipment that improve the quality of work and reduce the time required to construct it are valid business investments. Look for deals online and don't be afraid to consider second-hand merchandise.

The Value of Time

As a new business owner, you may not have the luxury of valuing your time as highly, but eventually you will face more demand for your products than you can produce on your own. Rather than allow your business to be limited, look for other ways to produce products. Your business will benefit and so will you. Decreasing the time you spend on repetitive, non-creative tasks will not only give you more time to do other things - it will also prevent boredom and burnout.

Cost of Materials

The search for lower cost supplies is an ongoing pursuit for jewelry designers. To keep costs down, buy wholesale whenever possible. Go in on orders with other people when the minimum order is too big for your needs. Shop estate sales and gem shows for lower prices and, when possible, substitute expensive materials with lower cost alternatives.

Wholesale and Bulk Purchases

Most jewelry suppliers extend deeper discounts to businesses than they do to the general public. Wholesale discounts range from 15% to 50% off regular retail prices. As a business owner, you won't have to pay sales tax on these purchases.

You will also save money when you buy in bulk because most suppliers offer discounts based on quantity. To buy wholesale, you will need to present your EIN number or business license (Chap. 9). A list of wholesale suppliers can be found in the back of the book on page 135.

Gem and jewelry shows are great for bulk and wholesale purchases. You should attend at least one show a year to stock up on well priced supplies and materials. You will need to present your EIN number, taxpayer number, and a business card for access to these shows. A list of gem and jewelry shows can be found on page 140.

Tucson Gem and Mineral Show

The Tucson Gem and Mineral Show is a two week event, held every year in February. With over 3,500 dealers and 40,000 visitors, it is the world's largest gem and jewelry show and is Tucson's biggest annual event.

In addition to the main show, there are over forty smaller shows, offering a massive range of products. You can shop for fossils, African art, jewelry books, tools, beads, gems, stones, and anything else related to the jewelry industry. A variety of workshops and classes are also available.

Here are a few tips for attending the show:
- Visit www.TGMS.org.
- Make hotel reservations well in advance.
- Scope out the shows you want to attend beforehand (this event can be overwhelming). You can download a show guide at www.TucsonShowGuide.com or pick one up at the Tucson airport when you arrive.
- Decide your budget and stick to it (it's very easy to overspend).
- Take advantage of busses and shuttles, which pick up at designated parking lots and stop at most shows.

Lower Cost Alternatives

Just last spring, I walked into Nordstrom wearing a pair of sterling silver and quartz earrings. While perusing the jewelry counters, I was approached by a sales person. She quickly presented a pair of earrings from the display and said, "it's so fun to see these acrylic earrings everywhere—these are just like the ones you have on." At first, I was indignant. My jewelry was *not* acrylic. My second reaction was shock when I saw the earrings were selling for $49.

How could plastic sell for so much? Often, people shopping for jewelry are more interested in the design than the quality of materials used to create it. When substitution does not sacrifice the design or overall quality, it may have only a small affect the asking price.

Lab Grown Gemstones

Lab grown gemstones are created in a controlled environment that mimics the way the stones are formed in nature. When it's finished, a lab grown stone is molecularly identical to one mined from the ground. Its crystal structures are chemically identical to a mined stone, and it has the same hardness on the Mohs scale.

High quality lab grown stones are an affordable and environmentally sensitive alternative to mined gemstones. For example, Rio Grande sells a mid-grade, 4mm ruby for $34.50, while their lab grown rubies sell for less than a dollar. Unless your niche is high end gem ware, you can often substitute with lab grown stones.

Though you should not advertise a lab grown stone as mined, most people cannot tell the difference with many types of stones, including diamonds.

Synthetic vs. Lab Grown

Don't confuse the word synthetic with lab grown. Though the words suggest the same meaning, synthetic can be anything other than mined. It can be lab grown, plastic, glass, resin, or any material other than a mined stone. A stone or gem labeled "lab grown" must meet the standards described in this chapter.

Silver Plating

Silver plated findings and beads cost much less than their sterling silver counterparts. Made of brass, steel, plastic, or some other material, the pieces are coated with a very thin layer of silver. When using silver plated items, make sure the base material is brass. Silver adheres well to brass and the weight of brass gives pieces a feeling of higher quality.

Before you purchase, always ask about the plating thickness and the base material. Silver plating is measured in microns. Aim for plating of at least four microns (one to three is too thin and will wear off). Closer to eight or ten is even better.

Unless you create heirloom quality pieces or have a niche in sterling silver, high quality silver plated beads and other findings are fine in many instances. One exception is silver plated ear posts and wires (they can irritate the skin around the earlobe). Use your own judgment on substitutions. Implement them only when they won't diminish the look and feel of the piece or the overall experience for the buyer.

Gold Filled

Because gold is so expensive, substituting gold filled for solid gold is a common practice. The last time I checked with my supplier, one ounce of 14k gold filled wire was $41 versus $600 for the solid gold wire. It's easy to see why many designers, as well as their customers, prefer gold filled.

Test Your Market

If you are unsure about using lower cost materials, start by introducing a few pieces to compare how well they sell against the rest of your line. If they don't do well, you have your answer. But more likely than not, you will find that jewelry made with less costly substitutions can sell just as well as those made with expensive materials.

In fact, a wider range of choices may even grow your customer base and increase sales. Remember, it's all right to use alternative materials; it's never okay to advertise them as the real thing.

Gold filled materials and findings contain a layer of gold that has been pressure bonded to another metal. The gold layer is thick enough to last for decades without showing wear.

Gold Plating

Gold plating has become increasingly common, and there is no reason you can't use it if you want to sell gold jewelry. Plating uses a much thinner coat of gold than gold filled and will wear off over time.

A gold plated piece that comes in contact with the skin will wear down where it is rubbed, so a gold plated ring, for example, won't hold up as long as a pair of gold plated hoops. Though it won't last long enough to become an heirloom, gold plated jewelry is widely accepted and is a desirable alternative to costlier choices.

11

Business Operations

As a business owner, you will be responsible for not only fabricating jewelry and interacting with customers but also for operating your business. Business operations are the day-to-day processes and functions of your business that take place behind the scenes. Though they work to improve your business and enhance the shopping experience, operations are generally invisible to the customer.

To run an effective business, you need to keep costs low, maintain the necessary inventory, and fulfill orders in a timely manner. They may not be the most glamorous part of a jewelry business, but these basic functions are crucial to success. For example, do you track your inventory closely enough to know when a theft has occurred? Are you doing anything to prevent theft? If so, is that system hindering sales?

115

Inventory control and theft prevention will save your business money, but they don't happen on their own. Managing your operations will be up to you. This chapter covers what you need to know to do it well.

Know Your Process

To improve efficiency and increase capacity, first outline your process. Name each step required to make and sell a piece of jewelry. Start at the beginning, with designing a piece and shopping for supplies. Summarize each step all the way through completing the sale and packaging the product.

This exercise will help you understand where your business may be vulnerable and where you can improve your approach. Perfecting your process will save you time and money while making your customers happy too. Here are some questions to ask yourself about your process:

- What are the biggest strengths to your process?
- Which steps require the most time to complete?
- Which steps are the most expensive?
- Which steps benefit the customer most?
- Where are areas for improvement?
- Which steps could be combined, eliminated, or outsourced?

Inventory

Without inventory, you have no way to generate income. Though you may have a small inventory when you first start your business, you should aim to increase it steadily. The more products you have, the more likely shoppers will find something they want. However, you shouldn't have more inventory than you know you can sell. Be sure you have a consistent way to maintain your inventory before you approach retail stores. If your inventory for re-orders is unreliable, stores will discontinue your line.

Let the questions below guide your inventory decisions:

- What is the minimum amount of inventory you need to have on hand for sales at parties and shows?
- How much inventory do you need to fulfill orders from shops and boutiques?
- How much money (and future business) do you stand to lose if you can't fulfill an order?
- How much is too much inventory?
- How do you track your inventory changes?
- Does your method indicate when an item is missing or unaccounted for?
- How will you know if a theft has occurred?

Theft Prevention

How will you prevent theft without hurting sales? You want your pieces to be accessible to potential customers but not so accessible that thieves target your jewelry. The biggest problem with theft arises at craft shows, public markets, and street fairs.

Greet and make eye contact with everyone who approaches your booth. This will not only improve sales—it will also discourage thieves. Shoplifters often take advantage of distracted vendors. Keep an eye out when you set up and take down you booth. Watch your jewelry closely. Never leave it unattended. If you need to use the restroom or take a break, arrange to have someone else watch over your jewelry while you're away.

Theft Proof Ring Display

1. If you use a traditional slotted ring display, drill a very small hole through the back of the display board behind each ring slot.

2. Tie a piece of string or fishing line around each ring. The string should be thin enough that customers can still try on the ring for size.

3. Thread the other end of the string through the slot and the corresponding hole.

4. Attach an anchor to the loose end of each string, or tie them all together in a knot on the backside of the display board.

5. This will allow the strings to be pulled back-and-forth through the display. People can try on the rings but can't walk away with them.

Journey of a Product

This section outlines the process of production, marketing, and the sale of a single item. It shows every step that a product goes through from the original design to the final destination.

Product Creation
1. Design the piece.
2. Build a prototype.
3. Wear the piece to test for comfort, look, and durability.
4. Determine how many to produce for the line.
5. Make an approximate determination on the price point to ensure it will be reasonable.
6. Make necessary modifications.
7. Approve the prototype.
8. Shop for the supplies and materials needed to produce the desired number.
9. Create a timeline and plan to construct the pieces.
10. Construct jewelry.

Product Marketing

1. Calculate wholesale and retail prices based on actual costs.
2. Create price tags and hang tags (if appropriate).
3. Work new item into display. If necessary, purchase or devise new display furniture.
4. Photograph and list item on Etsy.com.
5. Plan to sell item at trunk shows and fairs.

Order Fulfillment for Etsy.com Sales

1. Customer places an order and pays online.
2. Notification of the order is received.
3. Item is wrapped in tissue and placed in gift box.
4. Gift box and business card are placed in shipping box.
5. Item is weighed to determine postage.
6. Postage is created online and printed.
7. Postal pick up is scheduled for the following day.
8. Customer receives item 5-7 days after placing the order.

Order Fulfillment at Trunk Shows and Craft Fairs

1. Customer chooses an item to buy.
2. Invoice is written.
3. Customer contact information is collected.
4. Payment accepted in cash or check.
5. Item is packaged in a gift box.
6. Customer copy of invoice and a business card is included with the purchase.

Documentation

1. Record contact information collected from customers.
2. Retain receipts for purchased materials.
3. Retain a copy of the invoice for sales.
4. Record the number of items sold through each sales channel.

Order Fulfillment and Distribution

The process by which you respond to customer orders and purchases is called order fulfillment. You will probably use different methods to fulfill different types of orders. Mail order items, website sales, party sales, and wholesale orders from retailers each require their own variations on packaging and delivery preparation. A streamlined order fulfillment and distribution process for each sales channel will save you time and headaches.

- What is the ordering process for each of your sales channels?
- What are the terms of payment? Which forms of payment do you accept?
- Will items be made to order or will you maintain inventory to supply each purchase?
- How will you package items for the customer to carry away?
- How will you package items to be mailed?
- How will you collect and store shipping information?
- Will you include a business card or brochure with each sale?
- Will you charge for shipping? How much?
- Will you personally deliver wholesale orders when possible to strengthen relationships?
- What time frame will you guarantee for orders?
- Will you work with the post office or set up an account with UPS or FedEx?
- Do you have time to make trips to these shipping outlets or would you prefer they stop by for pick up?
- Will you insure shipments?

Shipping Short Cut

An online account with the United States Postal Service (USPS.com) allows you to pay online with a credit card, print the shipping label directly from your computer, and arrange for pick up at your home or place of business. This short cut will save you several hours a week. Additionally, the printed labels add a professional looking touch. All you need is a kitchen scale to weigh the packages and a printer for the labels.

Product Suppliers

You will probably have a few favorite sources you consistently buy from as well as some specialty suppliers that you use less often. Working with multiple suppliers to source your materials allows you to find the best prices for different items. Always be on the lookout for lower cost suppliers, including those overseas. Consider the following questions:

- Who are your suppliers?
- Have you made an effort to introduce yourself and get to know them?
- How will your business be affected if one of your materials becomes unavailable?
- Do you have a backup if a supplier falls through?

12

Tax Deductions

Once you make money, you have to pay taxes on your earnings. This chapter explains the tax issues you can expect to encounter as a small business owner as well as how to get the most from your tax deductions. If you do your own taxes, I recommend a program such as TurboTax or TaxCut (around $35) to ensure you haven't overlooked something. Check with your accountant if you are unsure about reporting or deducting.

There are five basic principles you need to know for taxes and deductions:

1. The payments received for jewelry sales need to be reported to the IRS.
2. You will owe the IRS money based on how much you earn each year.

3. You need to track your income, expenses, and profit for each year.
4. You may offset the money you owe the IRS by deducting expenses.
5. All expenses and deductions must be supported by a receipt or invoice.

Tax Reporting

Filing your taxes does not have to be difficult. At the end of the year, you will file forms with the IRS to report your earnings and expenses. If your business is a sole proprietorship or a partnership, you will report your business income and expenses on a Schedule C form and on your 1040 tax form.

If you have an LLC, you will file a 1065 tax form for your business. You will not pay taxes on that filing; it's just an administrative requirement. On your personal 1040 and Schedule C, you will report and pay taxes on any amount you personally withdrew from the LLC. If you withdrew nothing, you will not owe on your business earnings.

Tax Deductions

You can reduce the amount of money you owe the IRS by using tax deductions to decrease your taxable income. Tax deductions are expenses incurred as part of doing business and can be subtracted from your income at the end of the year. The IRS requires you to document all deductions with an invoice or receipt. To comply, you need to start documenting your expenses right away. Don't worry—it's much easier than you think.

Tax deductions are easy to track and easy to report. The IRS has a form (called a Schedule C) where you write in your expenses. Your tax payment is calculated once your expenses are subtracted from your income and your profit has been determined. Depending on your income and expenses, deductions can save you hundreds to thousands of dollars in tax payments.

Keep more of your hard earned money by taking advantage of the many tax benefits that are available to you as a small business owner. The list below includes the most common deductions for jewelry crafters.

Home Office, Studio, or Workshop

If you do most of your work at home, you probably have a space the IRS considers a home studio or office. A home studio can be an entire room in your home or just a portion of a room. If the room is used exclusively for work (not a spare bedroom), you can deduct the entire space. If you don't have a room all to yourself, you can still deduct the square footage of the space you use. If your home studio is part of a spare bedroom or a corner of a room, for example, determine the square footage of the space you use for your jewelry business.

Once you determine the square footage, divide that number by the square footage of your entire home. Say you live in 2000 square foot house and your workspace is ten feet by ten feet, or one-hundred square feet. Divide 100 by 2000 and you get .05, or 5%. This is the percentage of your total home expenses that can be deducted. In this example, it is 5% of the following home costs:

- Rent or mortgage related expenses (interest, home insurance, and real estate taxes) for the year.
- Condo fees paid for the year.
- Renters or homeowners insurance paid for the year.
- Electricity and utility bills for the year.

At first glance, 5% doesn't seem like much of a deduction until you apply it to thousands of dollars in home costs. For documentation, save copies of your electric and utility bills as well as insurance premiums, year-end mortgage statements, and rental agreements.

To avoid an administrative nightmare, set aside two boxes: one for your expense receipts and the other for your copy of sales invoices. At the end of the year, they will all be there waiting for you to add up and report.

Office Supplies

Highlighters, pens, staplers, envelopes, printer ink, paper, light bulbs, and anything else you need to maintain your day-to-day office operations are considered office supplies. These items are all deductible as long as you save the receipts.

Furniture

Need a new workbench or storage cabinet for your workspace? Be sure to keep the receipts so you can deduct the full cost. The IRS allows for a maximum of $250,000 (in 2008) in furniture deductions alone. Studio furniture can include:
- Desks
- Jewelers bench
- Workbench
- Tables
- Chairs
- File cabinets
- Shelves, cabinets, and storage items
- Lighting

Equipment and Tools

Equipment deductions aren't limited to the listed items below. For example, the purchase of a camera for the exclusive purpose of photographing pictures of your jewelry can be deducted. Purchased items must be used only for business purposes to qualify for IRS deductions. As always, you must have invoices or receipts for anything you deduct.

- Bench and jewelry tools
- Kilns, polishers, sand blasters, and other equipment
- Rotary tools and flex shafts
- Computers
- Printers
- Copiers
- Fax machines
- Scanners

Materials

All of the materials you buy to create your jewelry can be deducted as expenses for your business. It doesn't matter if you buy them wholesale, retail, through catalogs, or at shows. If you have a receipt, you can deduct the expense. Materials can include:

- Wire
- Metal
- Beads
- Findings
- Sandpaper
- Enamel
- Other materials used in your work

Education and Research

Whenever you attend a workshop or class to learn more about jewelry or a related topic, you can deduct the cost as business related education. If you attend speaking engagements, buy books, DVDs, or subscribe to journals or magazines, you can deduct the cost if the items are for research or education.

Sometimes education and research involves travel. If you travel to another city for a gem show or a class, for example, your travel expenses are deductible too.

Travel Related Expenses

When you travel away from home for business, all expenses related to overnight travel can be deducted. They include:

- Train, bus, and airline tickets
- Cab fare
- Hotel and lodging for overnight travel
- Tips for wait-staff, cabs, etc.
- Car rentals
- Phone calls made from the hotel or from payphones
- Dry-cleaning
- 50% of the cost of meals, even if the travel is not overnight

Overnight travel is defined as travel too far to conveniently return home at night. For example, a workshop or class in a nearby suburb of your city won't qualify for overnight travel deductions. On the other hand, a city two and a half hours away could be inconvenient for return, depending on your travel preferences. Travel expenses you can deduct include those you incur for:

- Buying materials
- Conducting sales
- Marketing
- Education
- Research

What happens when you mix business travel with leisure travel? If the trip is primarily for work, the normal deductions still apply, though you can't include non-work related

SELL YOUR JEWELRY

expenses. For example, lodging, meals, and travel expenses incurred during the leisure portion of your trip cannot be deducted. If you decide to stay in the town of travel for a couple of extra days, expenses from the extra days are not deductible. On the other hand, deductions for a one week trip to a city where you plan to work half a day can include only the expenses incurred for the work event. Travel, lodging, and meals for the entire one week trip are not deductible.

Auto and Transportation Expenses

You don't have to stay overnight to deduct everyday travel expenses. In fact, you don't even have to go far. Deductions can be taken for any type of work related transportation. Subway, bus, and cab fare can be deducted for work related outings.

Drive your own car? The easiest way to deduct auto expense is based on the miles you drive. Whether you are driving to the store to buy supplies or across town to a home party, your travel expenses are work related. If your workplace is your home, you can start counting the miles when you pull out of your driveway. Otherwise, you will start counting miles once you reach your first work related destination and stop when you reach the last one.

Keep a small date book in your car to record the distance you drive each day for work related activities. The IRS deduction is usually around $0.55 per mile. The deduction amount increases by a few cents each year.

Insurance Premiums

If you pay for your own health insurance, your premiums are deductible. The deduction does not apply if you are eligible for other forms of health care coverage through your employer or your spouse's employer.

Your total insurance deductions cannot exceed the total amount of your net profit earned. Save copies of your premiums for proof of the expense. Talk to your accountant if you are unsure about a particular deduction.

Other Expenses

To get the most from your tax deductions, read *Home Business Tax Deductions: Keep What You Earn,* by Stephen Fishman and Diana Fitzpatrick. You can also talk to your accountant. Other deductible expenses commonly incurred by jewelry designers include:

- Postage
- Long distance telephone calls
- A second phone line for work
- Subscriptions and memberships
- Legal and professional fees
- Half of your Social Security contributions
- Studio or storage rental
- Computer programs / Software

When in doubt about a deduction, ask your accountant for clarification. For every deduction you take, you must be able to prove the expense occurred with an invoice or receipt. As long as you stay within IRS guidelines and deduct honest expenses, you can keep more money in your pocket and pay less to the IRS. The IRS makes frequent changes to their requirements. Consult a professional for the most up to date information.

Gem and Jewelry Suppliers and Expos

Bead and Beading Suppliers

Fusion Beads
www.FusionBeads.com
Beads and findings

Shipwreck Beads
www.ShipWreckBeads.com
Beads and findings

Picard Beads
www.PicardBeads.com
Beads and findings

Beadalon
www.Beadalon.com
Beads and beading supplies

Fire Mountain Gems
www.FireMountainGems.com
Beads, gems, pearls

Soft Flex
www.SoftFlexCompany.com
Beads and beading supplies

Bally Bead Company
www.BallyBead.com
Beads and findings

Venetian Bead Shop
www.VenetianBeadShop.com
Glass beads

Casting Services

Sierra Pacific Casting
www.SierraPacificCasting.com
Casting service

Art Tech Casting Company
www.ArtTech.org
Casting service

Alpine Casting
www.AlpineCasting.com
Casting service

Prototype Casting
www.ProtCast.com
Casting service

Findings Suppliers

Eastern Findings
www.EasternFindings.com
Findings

Olympia Gold
www.OlympiaGold.com
Costume jewelry supplies

John Mathieu Fashion Jewelry Components
www.JewelryThings.com
Findings

CGM
www.cgmFindings.com
Beads, findings, tools

Gemstone Suppliers

New Era Gems
www.NewEraGems.com
Cut stones and crystals

AZ Gems
www.azGems.com
Crystals, beads, and gems

D & J Rare Gems
www.djRareGems.com
Fine and rare gem stones

General Suppliers

Rio Grande
www.RioGrande.com
Metal, tools, supplies, and beads

Santa Fe Jewelers Supply
www.sfjsSantaFe.com
Metal, tools, supplies, and beads

David H. Fell and Co.
www.dhfco.com
Metal refining, scrap reclaiming, and base metals

Hoover and Strong
www.HooverAndStrong.com
Refiner and manufacturer. Metal, tools, findings, supplies, and gems

Metalliferous
www.metalliferous.com
Metal, tools, supplies, and beads

Thunderbird Supply Company
www.ThunderbirdSupply.com
Metal, supplies, tools, beads, and stones

Stuller
www.Stuller.com
Metal, supplies, tools, beads, and stones

Glass and Enamel Suppliers
Thompson Enamel
www.ThompsonEnamel.com
Glass enamel

Schlaifer's Enameling Supplies
www.Enameling.com
Glass enamel for metal

Bullseye Glass
www.Bullseye-Glass.com
Glass, tools, and supplies for fusing and blowing

Ed Hoys International
www.EdHoy.com
Glass, tools, and supplies for stained glass, lampwork, fusing, and blowing

Delphi Glass
www.DelphiGlass.com
Glass supplies and precious metal clay supplies

138

Metal Clay Suppliers

PMC Connection
www.pmcConnection.com
Metal clay, tools, and supplies

Cool Tools
www.CoolTools.us
Metal clay, tools, and supplies

Art Clay World
www.ArtClayWorld.com
Metal clay, tools, and supplies

Other Specialty Suppliers

Gesswein
www.Gesswein.com
Tools and supplies

Blake Brothers
www.BlakeBros.com
Sterling silver wholesaler

Reactive Metals Studio
www.reactivemetal.com
Misc. metals like nobium and titanium

Red Sky Plating
www.RedSkyPlating.com
Metal plating and surface applications (sandblasting)

Hauser and Miller
www.HauserAndMiller.com
Metal supplies, fabrication, and refinery

Shows and Expos

International Gem and Jewelry Show
www.InterGem.com
A traveling show that sells huge volumes of gems, beads, and jewelry findings. See website for the schedule.

Tucson Gem and Mineral Show
Tucson Arizona
www.TGMS.org
The world's largest gem and jewelry show. A few of the other shows in Tucson that coincide with it are listed here:

Rapa River Gem and Mineral Show
American Indian Expo
Rio Grande Catalog in Motion
Arizona Mineral and Fossil Show
The Bead Renaissance
The Best Bead Show
The Whole Bead Show
Mineral and Fossil Co-op
Tucson Southwest Jewelry, Gem, and Bead
Pueblo Gem and Mineral Show
AKS Gem Show
Granada Avenue Mineral Show
African Art Village
Jewelry, Gem, and Mineral Expo
To Bead True Blue
Five Minerals International
Create Your Own Style with Swarovski
Manning House Mansion Bead Show
Tucson Westward Look Mineral Show
Tucson Bead Show

Index

A

accounting, 94
alternative materials, 110-113
appearance, 7, 8, 26, 31, 49, 72
appointments, 81-82
attitude, 26

B

bank accounts, 32, 89, 93-94
booths, 76-78, 102, 117
boutiques, 11, 13, 15, 26, 28, 31, 34, 40, 49, 79-83, 100, 117
bulk purchases, 11, 102, 105, 107
business Cards, 8, 28, 71, 78, 83, 96,
business license, 5, 89, 91-92, 93, 94, 106, 108,
business Name, 27
business structure, 90-91
buyer, Focus, 13
buying Sensitivities, 18, 21

C

cash, 31-33, 78, 80
casting, 96, 105,
checks, 21, 31, 32, 39, 93
consignment, 85-87,
contact information, 27, 28, 31, 35, 83
cost of materials, 38, 41, 42, 106, 108
cost of time, 40, 105
craft shows, 76
credit cards, 21, 32, 94
custom orders, 4, 28, 31, 34-35

D/E

deals, 18, 19, 36, 62
demographics, 15, 4, 18, 22
descriptive tags, 48, 50
display Materials, 48-89

display, 7, 8, 21, 35-36, 47, 49, 50, 64, 65, 77, 78, 85, 97
distribution, 122
Employer Identification Number, 93-94, 108
Etsy.com, 71-73
expensive materials, 19, 44, 51, 108,

F/G

fairs, 5, 33, 38, 50, 76-79
farmers markets, 76-79
finished pieces, purchasing, 106-107
forms of payment, 31-33, 60
general partnership, 90-91
goals, 98-102
gold filled, 52, 112-113
gold plating, 113
guarantee, 33-34, 122

H/I

hiring help, 71, 94, 107
home party, 32, 41-42, 50, 64-65, 131
increasing value, 42-45
inventory, 4-5, 63, 72, 81, 86, 115, 117-118
invoices, 28-29, 78, 126

L/M/N

lab grown stones, 110-111
lifestyle, of customer, 19
Limited Liability Company, 91
line Sheet, 31
market value, 37, 38
markets, 76-79
minimums, 79-80
niche, 7-13, 72, 77

O

open house, 32, 50, 59, 60-65
order forms, 28-29, 65,

order fulfillment, 122-123
Overhead costs, 37, 38, 39, 83

P

packaging, 21, 35-36, 48, 97, 122
packing list, 78
pay yourself, 39
PayPal, 32-33
perceived value, 25, 42-45, 47
policies, 21, 25 31-35, 80, 81
presentation, 35-36, 45-46, 47-57
price sheet, 30, 31, 79, 82
price tags, 36, 62, 67,
pricing, 37-45, 79
profit, 37, 39,
promotions, 18, 19, 36, 62
ProPay, 32
psychology, 19
purchasing patterns, 20

Q/R

quality, 3, 21, 35, 37, 38, 43, 47, 71, 76, 107, 110, 111
recycled materials, 51
retail outlets, see boutiques
return policy, 33, 81

S

sales tax number, 92
sales tax, 89, 92, 108
sample invitation, 61
Shrinky Dinks, 2
silver plating, 111-112
sole proprietorship, 90
start-up costs, 95-97
store orders, 34
strategic alliances, 102
street fairs, 5, 33, 38, 50, 76-79
style, 3, 7-14, 47-52,
suppliers, 123

T-Z

target customer description, 22
target customer, 16-24
tax deductions, 125-132
tax reporting, 126
terms of payment, 80, 122
theft prevention, 116-118
tiered pricing, 44
trunk shows, 5, 33, 40, 83-85
Tucson Gem Show, 109
wholesale, 30, 31, 34, 40-42, 79-83, 108
workplace sales, 34, 65-67
workspace, 38, 94-95

Breinigsville, PA USA
21 January 2011
253825BV00004B/44/P